How to Prepare Your Portfolio

A Guide for Students
and Professionals

By Ed Marquand

How to Prepare Your Portfolio

Art Direction Book Company, New York

Library of Congress Catalog Card Number: 81-66881
ISBN: 0-910158-69-X (cloth)
ISBN: 0-910158-70-3 (paper)

Printed in the United States of America

Published by
ART DIRECTION BOOK COMPANY
10 East 39th Street
New York, New York 10016

Edited By: Laurence Oberwager

To Kerry, Karen, Dolph, Toni, and Roger

ACKNOWLEDGEMENTS

A number of people have contributed to this book and I would like to express my appreciation for their help. They include Jeremy Kotas, Dugald Stermer, Jules Ann Hawes, Taj Diffenbaugh Worley, Toni Hollander, and Cindy Ford of the Design Works, and Jim Cheetham who all contributed work to be photographed for this book. I would also like to thank Andrew Addkison, Jack Kramer, Susan Rush, and Dora Williams for their advice and suggestions. Sondra Robertson deserves thanks for her aid in preparing the manuscript, as does Kathy Doty for her help in the photography of this book. Finally, I'm especially grateful to Diane Hines for her fine editorial assistance and encouragement.

Contents

Deciding what kind of artist you are. What you want your portfolio to do. Compiling and selecting art and verbal information. Selecting a physical format. Organizing your portfolio thematically and graphically. Constructing your portfolio.

Gathering, evaluating, and selecting artwork. Photographing oversized work. Evaluating the presentation process. Designing and assembling the portfolio.

Introduction

This book is about portfolios: how to plan them; how to design them; how to display artwork by reproducing it both graphically and photographically; how to organize and physically assemble portfolios; and, finally, how to use them to get the assignment or position that you seek.

A portfolio is a collection of visual information. Simple enough. However, a portfolio can be much more than that. It can be a tool to use in obtaining a job. It can be a diary or journal of images—a reference source of ideas for the artist to use in his work. It might be a document or it could give testimony to a profession or strong interest. A good portfolio is usually a collection of visual information about the work of a particular artist, graphically well presented, containing enough written verbal information to help explain what the artwork alone can't.

Some artists and designers prefer to think of their portfolios as books about themselves and the work they do. Perhaps this approach may make the task of organizing your portfolio more manageable.

A portfolio is really a book, hand assembled, that has a specific purpose and that will be seen by a specific group of people. Like any book, it can be well-organized, helpful, informative, well-crafted, and complete. But, as with any book, it can be poorly organized, distracting, uninteresting, too long or too short, sloppy, and insignificant. Given interesting artwork, some time and thought, and careful craftsmanship, however, any artist or designer can put together a portfolio that shows off his work to its best advantage.

This book discusses three different types of portfolios that all artists and designers can use: personal, professional, and documentary. However, the major portion of the book is devoted to the creation of a professional portfolio.

An artist or designer needs a professional portfolio because he must compete with an enormous number of very talented and creative people who are working, studying, showing, and selling their artwork and ideas. Artists, no matter how talented, often lack the specific technical knowledge and skills needed to put together a portfolio that successfully represents their work. This book was written to provide the artist with such knowledge and skill.

This book includes a variety of techniques for assembling professional portfolios that are not known to many artists and designers. These techniques were selected for their broad application and usefulness, no matter what type of art, craft, or design the artist is creating. None of the techniques are too difficult to master with a little time, practice, or (if you want someone to do the work for you) money.

The section on photography and its range of applications for artists and designers is included to help persons who are essentially non-photographers. Also included is information on process camera techniques, frequently used by graphic designers, that could be just as helpful to other kinds of artists and designers.

Since so many artists live in small towns away from large metropolitan areas, and since some of the supplies and services mentioned in this book may not be readily available locally, a list of suppliers and their addresses has been included so that you can more easily order your supplies by mail.

Finally, keep in mind that there is an element not covered in this book that really makes your portfolio; it's your creativity. With it, and with the suggestions in this book, you will be able to make your portfolio an exceptional representation of your professional abilities.

1.
Personal, Professional, and Documentary Portfolios

Essentially, there are three different kinds of portfolio: personal, professional, and documentary. Let's consider each one in turn.

PERSONAL PORTFOLIOS

A personal portfolio is a visual diary: a journal of sketches, notes, and ideas. It can also be a collection of technical information: images and photographs from other sources like magazines, brochures, and instruction sheets. The subject matter, or content, in a personal portfolio can be as diverse as the artist's or designer's interests. The artist assembles his personal portfolio to better organize information that's important to him and can assist him in his art. His needs determine the form the personal portfolio will take.

Many artists get ideas from photographs, articles they've seen, or even doodles they've done during stray, inspired moments. These loose bits of visual information are, in effect, notes that can help them recall ideas and images necessary to their creative work. When properly organized, these can be the beginning of a valuable personal portfolio. When left unorganized, such visual information becomes stacks of scraps, awkward to handle and difficult to use, and their value to the artist is minimal. Some unusually well-organized artists have elaborate picture files, cross-referenced and cataloged. Most artists don't require anything that complex. There are several simple ways to file, or assemble, these notes.

Assembling a Personal Portfolio

Storing your notes, clippings, and photos in 8½ x 11" three-ring binders works nicely if they are small enough to be glued onto pieces of heavy paper about the weight of index cards. Larger clippings can be folded and then glued on the paper for a foldout arrangement.

Index-card-weight stock is firm enough to take the glue and clippings, yet thin enough so that it doesn't take up all the space in your notebook. It's also considerably less expensive than art paper, illustration board, or bristol board, especially if you buy it in quantity. A terrific (and cheap) source of good papers are the paper supermarkets that paper companies

FIGURE 1. This photographer's personal portfolio is made up of photos and images from periodicals that interest him. Glued to sheets of 8½ x 11" index paper and inserted into a three-ring binder, these photographs are more easily accessible and valuable than if they had been left in the magazines from which they came.

are opening in large metropolitan areas. They are usually set up to sell single sheets or entire reams from a broad selection of papers.

If 8½ x 11″ is a little to small for your notes and clippings, or if you don't really want them bound in a notebook, consider glueing these notes on legal-size (8½ x 14″) index-card stock instead. After you have glued them to the cards, file each category or group of notes into a legal-size manilla folder which can then be stored in cardboard boxes, crates, or regular metal file cabinets. No matter how you decide to store your clippings, sketches, and notes, remember that they will last longer if you mount them first.

If you photograph your notes, sketches, articles, lecture demonstrations, or procedures, your photos and slides can be easily filed as well. Appendix II describes some practical photo files.

Once you discover a file system that works for you, you may find that you're collecting and filing more notes and pictures, and using the information from them more frequently. As your personal portfolio system grows, it will become an important reference book—which is exactly what it should be.

Specific Uses for a Personal Portfolio

A designer may be particularly interested in the uses of color in interiors. By collecting unusually fine examples of color use—or even unusually poor examples—and combining them with his own notes on

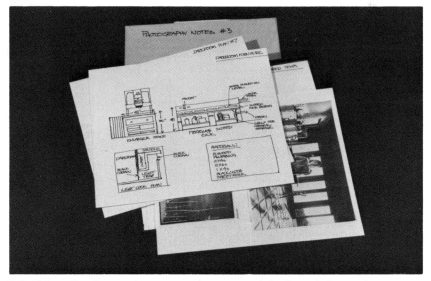

FIGURE 2. This photographer prefers making notes and sketches and glueing photos on 10 x 12″ sheets of white card stock and storing them in old photo paper boxes. Plans, technical notes, and experiment results are easily retrieved using this system.

the subject, the designer can accumulate a collection of information more valuable to him than any textbook on the subject.

A photographer, tearing and saving photos from recent art and photography periodicals, can put together a portfolio of information or images he finds personally inspiring or technically helpful, which can be far more useful to him than a stack of the same magazines gathering dust in his studio.

Artists and designers involved in current advances in their fields should remember that information published in magazines tends to be more up-to-date than information from books. This is because it takes longer to produce and distribute a book than a magazine or brochure. Some contemporary art and design books are never published for this reason; the content could be outdated by the time the book is finally on the market. Making your own books or file systems from magazine photos and articles can be a sensible solution to this problem.

As a craftsperson or sculptor, you may be accumulating information on techniques or processes to help you in your work. Incorporating this information into a personal portfolio allows you to keep your notes, sketches, working drawings, and results at hand. A good record of your experiences with these processes will prevent you from having to repeat an experiment because you've forgotten the results from the first time you tried it. Even a primitive effort to organize the information that's important to you will save you time and hassle.

Other uses of personal portfolios can be more evocative in purpose. Most active and inquisitive artists and designers run occasional visual experiments purely to satisfy their own curiosity. An illustrator, for example, may have a sculpture in progress in his studio. A photographer might be experimenting with fantasy effects. An environmental designer may design jewelry as a side interest. A fashion designer might start weaving tapestries. Since these kinds of activities are related to the artist's visual and creative sense—but aren't professional enough or even appropriate for his professional portfolio—they should be included in his personal portfolio.

Occasionally, an artist will even discover that it's an unusual combination of interests or talents that makes him an especially creative individual. Keeping the results of his efforts in a personal portfolio of this kind can evolve into a source of encouragement, spurring the experimenting designer or artist on to new and more interesting endeavors, which, given time, could eventually evolve or overlap into professional activities. The tapestry-weaving fashion designer may start selling tapestries. The photographer may stumble onto a specific technique at which he is especially competent. Even after a designer or artist chooses a specialty, he needs to remain open to new developments in his own creative life; and a personal portfolio may help him to do just that.

PROFESSIONAL PORTFOLIOS

The professional portfolio is created for specific purposes and is effective when it's designed as a communication aid. It must fulfill not only the needs of the designer, but those of his potential clients or employers as well. The professional portfolio should be tailored to meet specific requirements of the situation: finding a job, getting into school, applying for a grant, entering a competition, looking for freelance work, or finding gallery representation.

Given the volatile nature of personalities and temperaments in the art and design professions, it's not unusual for a mid-career professional artist (perhaps an artist who has worked for the same client for a number of years) to suddenly find himself in need of a portfolio to help him find another job or new freelance work. Unless he has kept good samples of the work he has done, he may well find himself unable to put together an accurate representation of his abilities and experience. So, professional portfolios are just as important to professionals as they are to recent art school graduates.

Portfolios play an important part in the business of art and design. New clients are wise to request portfolio presentations from photographers, interior designers, or graphic artists before contracting work from them.

From the other side, as an artist or designer contracting work, you too have the right to see the portfolios of the people you are considering hiring. As an interior designer, for example, you would want to see the work of a professional interior photographer before you sign a contract with him to photograph a job you are working on. Why? You want to see evidence that the photographer you are about to hire is indeed familiar with the kind of work you need done. Since you can realistically expect to receive quality similar to that you have been shown, you may decide not to hire someone after seeing his work.

As a professional in the visual arts, you will need a portfolio to show your skills in your chosen profession, and you should also expect to see the portfolios of those you intend to hire. It's about the best way to avoid disappointments, misunderstandings, costly mistakes, wasted time, and attorney's fees.

Also keep in mind that if you are applying for a job in art or design and you are *not* asked to show samples of your work, you should be immediately suspicious. Any employer so uninterested in your past work will probably not be interested in your creative abilities in the future. He may have a job so routine and repetitive that he thinks anyone can learn it, or it may be a position with virtually no design standards. Few good designers do well in those situations.

The mechanics of selecting artwork and assembling and presenting a professional portfolio will be discussed in detail in Chapters 2 – 8.

DOCUMENTARY PORTFOLIOS

The documentary portfolio is especially helpful to those who want to show a single project, process, or artistic activity, as opposed to a collection of finished objects or pieces of artwork. A documentary portfolio can be particularly successful when it's used to supplement a professional portfolio. A large design project that is too complicated to explain in your regular portfolio can be given the space and attention it deserves in a documentary portfolio.

Two examples: First, let's say you are a graphic designer working on small or medium-size design projects and you are suddenly awarded a contract for an enormously complex annual report, requiring a vast amount of time, research, coordination, and supervision. A separate documentary portfolio about the entire project, composed of photographs, written documentation and descriptions, timetables, budgets, a conclusion and evaluation of the effort, perhaps bound as a small book, would be an impressive document by itself. As a non-attached supplement to your professional portfolio, it would be a wonderfully comprehensive example of your talents.

Next, as an interior designer in charge of a massive conversion project, like creating a stylish restaurant from a delapidated barn, a documentary portfolio would help you explain the details of this project

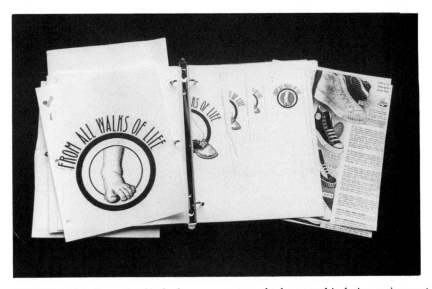

FIGURE 3. This three-ring binder keeps concept roughs for a graphic design assignment grouped and organized. The designer may show this documentary portfolio to the client to illustrate progression of his ideas, or he may only keep it for his reference files.

more clearly. It might begin as a project description with lots of "before" photos and "after" floorplans. Photos of the work in progress and in order would come next, followed by a budget and notes on some of the technical details not apparent in the photographs. At the end of this documentary portfolio there would be some excellent photographs of the finished project.

Architects and designers who take the time to assemble documentary portfolios of such major projects find them helpful not only in supplementing their professional portfolios but also in planning subsequent major projects. The documentary portfolio helps show how much time, effort, and money is involved in big projects—something which few clients are aware of. Individuals or firms that hire designers to take on major projects are wildly optimistic about how long a project should take and how much it should cost. The information and experience gained in your first project, properly compiled into a documentary portfolio, is much more valuable to you if you can communicate it to a client in a subsequent project.

To put together a good documentary portfolio, keep careful records and photographs of your work as it progresses. After your project is finished, organize all of the photos and records you've kept so that they tell the story of your work from start to finish. Then assemble the portfolio using the methods and techniques for professional portfolios discussed in the following chapters. Also refer to the section on permanent binding in Chapter 5 for ideas especially appropriate to finished documentary portfolios.

2.
Six-Step Plan for a Professional Portfolio

Preparing a professional portfolio is a difficult task because you're trying to convince someone that the work you've previously done qualifies you for the type of work he wants. He will probably be looking for specific points in your work that fit his requirements, so you must somehow emphasize those points or aspects of your work. The entire situation can become a complicated matching game; but the more care you take in analyzing the needs of a prospective employer, and in planning your portfolio accordingly, the more effective and successful your portfolio will be.

Since the training, experience, and perceptions of artists and designers are so singular, and since the jobs they apply for are so diverse, it's not possible to present one, specific outline of what makes a perfect portfolio. There is, however, a six-step plan that should simplify the task of putting together your professional portfolio. It's logical, practical, and appropriate for any artist or designer, whatever his work.

SIX-STEP PLAN

1. Decide what kind of artist or designer you are.
2. Decide what you want your portfolio to do for you.
3. Compile and select your artwork and verbal information.
4. Select a physical format for your portfolio.
5. Organize your work thematically and graphically.
6. Convert the artwork into a size to fit your portfolio format; assemble the graphic materials and tools you'll need; and, finally, construct your portfolio.

Step 1:   What Kind of Artist Are You?

The better an artist or designer knows his work, and knows how he works, the more likely he is to pursue the kind of work that will keep him excited and interested in his chosen profession. Coming to know your work is not an automatic process; it requires serious self-evaluation and, in some cases, criticism from collegues. For the most helpful kind of portfolio, though, the artist must see his work and direction clearly so he can illustrate those qualities that are going to help him reach his goals.

Start by writing a list of skills and talents you have. Carefully select the abilities you have an unusual talent for, and those you enjoy doing the most. Next, list those skills that you do a little less well, but still enjoy. The last list should be made up of skills you have, but do not enjoy at all.

Using these lists as a guide, pull out samples of the kinds of artwork you listed, good and bad, and evaluate them all: the samples of the work you want to do, as well as those you don't want to do. Judge each piece against similar, professionally accepted work. Try to know where you stand within you profession. Are you consistently good, or only occasionally excellent? Are you actually much better at what you dislike doing than at what you want to do? Why? If you find it difficult to judge the work for yourself, ask for the opinions of collegues, instructors, or friends whose judgement and candor you respect. Form opinions about the work you do.

Perhaps you see that you're a good generalist, skilled at many kinds of artistic tasks. Perhaps you see that you're a specialist. Are you too specialized within your field? Too general? Do you like most of your work equally, or are you wildly excited by some of it, and blase about the rest? Are there traits in your work that you strongly dislike? In other words, try to answer the question, "Why do I work the way I do?" Then think of how your answer is going to affect your career in the

11

future and your portfolio right now; for while these considerations will remain throughout your career, they're especially important when you begin to select the work you'll show in your portfolio.

Step 2:   What Do You Want Your Portfolio To Do?

The first basic function of the portfolio is to protect artwork in an attractive and organized manner. The second is to provide you with a communication aid, to help you in your career by clearly showing examples of your skills. Whether you approach your career with long- or short-term goals, you can design your portfolio so that it helps you reach them. Here are some examples:

1. Eventually, you want to be in charge of a small graphic department and you hope to work up to that job from a lower position. In your portfolio, you'll want to show a wide range of talents and skills right from the start to prove that you're capable and interested in more than a specialized job.
2. Say that you would eventually like to do editorial cartooning exclusively but you have a stack of technical illustrations. A technical illustration portfolio is not going to speed you to the work you really want to do; so make your portfolio reflect the type of artist you are or want to be.
3. If, as a photographer, you know you're going to need a dozen or so freelance assignments in the next month, design your portfolio so that you're showing very recent work to help emphasize the speed and deadlines with which you can work.
4. Art galleries usually schedule one-person shows many months in advance. They're less concerned with speed and more concerned with consistent artistic quality and thoughtfulness in your work. A portfolio showing that you can "crank them out like crazy" may impress a warehouse gallery that sells artwork by the square foot, but it won't impress any first-class gallery.
5. On the other hand, the production potter makes money by being both fast and consistent, so a helpful portfolio for him would be one that showed both of these abilities.
6. The illustrator who wants to work in many different styles should be showing a portfolio of all his favorite styles so that his potential clients don't peg him to just one kind of treatment.

Look ahead in your career and use your portfolio to help you reach your goals. Again, make sure your portfolio covers all of the kinds of work you are looking for, but be sure not to include types of work that you don't want to do in the future.

Unless you're asked to show very specific samples of your work, it's usually best to prepare a portfolio showing a range of your abilities. This is especially important for the artist or designer who hasn't chosen a specialty and needs to gain working experience in many areas. When you show a potential employer that you are capable of several kinds of work, it may make you more employable since it shows that you're capable of picking up new skills quickly. If you're after specific and very specialized positions or work, it would be wise only to show work that directly relates to your specialty.

If you're looking for a full-time permanent job with a company, show continuous involvement in your profession. When you go through your artwork, select a few samples that cover a long time span to verify your experience, but let the bulk of your portfolio consist of current work. A portfolio with little recent work but lots of old work indicates that the artist or designer hasn't done much in the field lately and may be out of touch.

If you are applying for regular employment, your resume is the place to show that you're a good, reliable employee. But this type of information is less important for a freelance artist or designer, because companies want to know about a freelancer's ability to fulfill an assignment—not about his ability to fit into an office situation.

Step 3: What to Include in Your Portfolio: Compiling and Selecting Art and Verbal Information

When you have decided what you want your portfolio to do, your next task is to go through all of your artwork and select the best examples of the kind of work you want to show. Compile and select examples of your work carefully; this will be the most important task, because your work is the "heart" of your portfolio.

If you're looking for work as a technical illustrator, some "exploded parts" drawings would be entirely appropriate, while inspired abstract sketches would not. If you're a fine artist looking for a gallery to show your intaglio prints, don't bother including color theory exercises you did as an art student. Select work that is similar in content, media, or technique to the work you want to obtain.

If you have work that's appropriate but low on quality, consider redoing it to bring it up to a higher standard. It's always safer to leave out work that you know is poor quality since it only detracts from your good work.

Also, be sure to include in your selection the full range of work you can do within your specialty. A graphic artist looking for a job should include a few brochures, a few advertisements, and some logos and letterheads, rather than showing only logos or only letterheads.

The commercial photographer going after a broad market needs a selection of product shots, portraits, posed-model and action shots—not just a single kind of photograph.

A sculptor should show the full range of materials and scale in his work. An illustrator should display the variety of styles and treatments he likes to use—from tight renderings to loose, spontaneous line drawings.

For suggestions on the content—or type of art—to include in a portfolio for a specific profession, see Chapter 7.

Verbal Information — In addition to artwork, you must consider your verbal, or written, information—how much to include and how to present it—when organizing and designing your portfolio. Your verbal information should explain what your artwork alone cannot. It may consist of captions on photographs, subject-divider headings, a resume, and that's all. Be careful not to rely too heavily on verbal information; if you do it will weaken the message of your artwork.

A good way to determine how much verbal information your portfolio needs is to lay out on the floor all your artwork in the order in which you want to arrange it in the portfolio. Pretend that you are an interviewer looking at your work for the first time. Try to imagine what your artwork alone would communicate to a stranger if you weren't there. Then try to think of what else the artwork needs to get its message across. The less it needs the better. (See Chapter 6.)

Step 4: Selecting a Physical Format

There are many formats for portfolios, each with its own set of advantages and disadvantages. You should examine the work you have selected to show and carefully consider how you'll be making your portfolio presentations. These two factors—the physical nature of your work and the method in which you'll present it—will determine your portfolio's format.

Most artists need a well-organized portfolio that they can easily carry with them to show new clients, agents, galleries, or potential employers. It should be durable and compact, yet large enough so that details in the artwork are clearly evident. For specific information on binders and other materials for portfolios, see Chapter 4.

Binder vs. Loose-Artwork Format — If the artwork needs additional verbal information and must be captioned or is in any way delicate or fragile, a ringed binder is the simplest way to protect the work in an organized manner. (Loose pieces of art, as opposed to those that are mounted, are difficult to caption, and they are always more susceptible to wear, fingermarks, spilled coffee, and other potential dangers.) A ringed binder also allows you flexibility in your portfolio presentation. If, after talking to your interviewer for a few minutes, you can sense that he wants to dash through your artwork, you can simply hand him your organized and graphically well-designed ring binder. Then, you can sit and field his questions or comments, while he leafs through it.

A portfolio of loose pieces of artwork is most effective when you are making the presentation yourself. If you know you will be expected to present and explain your work yourself, as you show it, consider the "loose-artwork" type of portfolio. If you know you will need captions for your work, or if you have to mail your portfolio and won't be able to explain your work in person, stick to a binder format.

The Storyboard Portfolio — A storyboard portfolio is a collection of random-size artwork mounted on a uniform size of backing board, collated into the order in which the boards will be shown. This is a good way to present your work to several people at the same time while maintaining a specific order or sequence to the artwork. A typical storyboard format might be ten or fifteen 20 x 30", or smaller, illustration or mat boards, each arranged with photos, drawings and large type indicating in broad terms the information you are explaining as you flip through each panel. Use only one side of the board for displaying your information.

FIGURE 4. *Individual pieces of matboard, in this case cut to an 11 x 14" format, have graphic samples mounted on them. This allows the designer to hand individual boards to an interviewer, thereby directing attention to each individual piece. If you are speaking about your work during an interview, this is a good format.*

Mailable Portfolios — Some artists and designers mail their portfolios to other cities and thus aren't able to personally present them. This requires a portfolio that is completely self-contained, without overlays, flip-up artwork, or special oddly constructed packages that require any skill or effort to manipulate. Captions and other verbal material should be complete. Samples, resumes, or photos that you want the receiver to retain for his files should be put in an envelope that's clearly marked as such. That way the receiver isn't as likely to remove some of the artwork that you want to keep.

Always enclose a stamped, self-addressed envelope or package to encourage the prompt return of your portfolio.

Selecting a Size — A convenient rule of thumb to use when deciding how large a page format you need for your portfolio is this: If most or all of your artwork is large or even environmental in scale—and must be photographed to be included in your portfolio anyway—then you can use a small binder like an 8½ x 11" three-ring notebook.

If you want something a bit larger, try 11 x 14", another common photo-enlargement size, which is reasonably priced compared to larger sizes. If 11 x 14" is too expensive for you, stick to the much cheaper 8½ x 11" size, or the even cheaper 8 x 10" format; but don't design your portfolio for photos smaller than 8 x 10" or it will begin to look like a snapshot album, and you will undoubtedly lose important detail in your prints.

As you're designing your page format, remember that spending, say, $12.00 for a custom color print may not sound like much, but if you need fifteen different enlargements made, your photo lab bill will come close to $200.00, which may be far more than your budget allows.

So, if you have to photograph your artwork to bring it down to a practical portfolio size, you will probably decide to use a three-ring 8½ x 11" binder or an 11 x 14" toothed binder, or a similarly sized storyboard format.

On the other hand, remember that original flat artwork is always more impressive than photographs of the work. If your work is small enough to fit into a reasonably sized portfolio, measure the largest piece and select a binder to fit it. If the bulk of your work is small but a few pieces are too large for the binder, photograph them and have prints made to fit the size of the smaller original artwork.

While original artwork is preferable to photos, there is a limit to how large your binder should be. An 18 x 24" binder opens to over 24 x 36", which is about as much space as an interviewer can be expected to clear from his desktop. If you insist on using a larger binder than that, you run the risk of creating a nuisance during an interview.

Whichever format you select for your portfolio, keep its size in mind when you make new artwork. If you do a lot of work, select a size and format that allows you to frequently edit and add to your portfolio without disrupting its basic format and its existing artwork. Since a professional portfolio should not be a complete collection of every piece of artwork you have ever made but rather a sampling of the best of your career, a flexible format that will allow you to exchange samples of artwork quickly will be more useful to you.

For example, if you're a graphic designer whose specialty is magazine advertisements, and you do a good number of them a year, you will probably want to replace the older ads with more recent ones the following year. By maintaining a flexible format, you can have a collection of your artwork in your portfolio that grows and changes with your career.

Recent students and graduates new to the professional scene will probably have mostly student work in their portfolios. There's nothing wrong with showing student work, as long as you gradually replace it with pieces done as your professional career progresses.

The recent graduate's portfolio format, then, should be very flexible; so select a format size compatible with the work you will be doing as a professional. A flexible size and format allows you to quickly and simply shift the emphasis and contents of your portfolio, so as to make it more appropriate for a particular client or interviewer.

Step 5: Organizing Your Portfolio Thematically and Graphically

After you've decided which artwork you want to include and what kind of binder and format will be most appropriate for it, you can start to organize and design your professional portfolio.

Pay close attention to the organization of your work. A prospective client isn't likely to be impressed by your organizational ability if the portfolio you show him is a disheveled mess, chock full of crumpled paper, dog-eared artboards, and wadded-up tear sheets. Your work should be arranged in a logical order, and should progress evenly, so that an interviewer can make the transition smoothly from one aspect of your work to the next.

Organizational Approaches

There are many different ways to arrange the work in your portfolio. You can use reverse chronological order, beginning with your latest work; you can group your work by medium used; or you can separate it into commercial work versus fine, or artistic, work. But, the best kind of organization for your portfolio depends on your work and your needs.

Some fine artists, interior designers, and craftsmen like to arrange their work in chronological order when there is a need to show an obvious long-term development or stylistic change in the work. On the other hand, it may be more logical to divide your work according to the materials used. For example, a group of wash paintings followed by a series of pen and inks followed by pencil drawings might be more effective than a hodge-podge of the three techniques. Then again, perhaps subject matter is a more obvious way to divide the work, with all figure drawings separated from watercolor studies.

A photographer might separate his commercial, product photographs from his more artistic photographs, since they usually differ in purpose and treatment. An interior designer might separate commercial, residential, and institutional interiors. However you decide to group the work, keep the categories broad and general so that you never have more than a few divisions in your portfolio.

If your art and design training is diverse, and your abilities broad, you might break down the examples you show by field rather than specialty. Perhaps it's more appropriate to have separate sections on graphics, illustration, and photography. Or sculpture, ceramics, and jewelry. Establishing a basic structure, or organization, gives your work a sense of unity within the portfolio, no matter how eclectic the individual pieces of artwork may seem.

You can make the contents of your portfolio more meaningful to someone unfamiliar with the way you work by showing, through step-by-step illustrations or photos, how you actually developed an art or design project. (Such a step-by-step section would be similar to a documentary portfolio as described in the Introduction, but it would be part of your professional portfolio.) Let's say you were awarded a commission to build a public sculpture. You could quickly show techniques you used—techniques not readily apparent in the finished piece—by photographing the steps in the sculpture's design and construction, and presenting the photographs in sequence. In a graphic design portfolio, you could show in a few pages the process involved in creating a corporate-identity program by including some roughs of your original ideas, a comprehensive, and, finally, a few of the finished printed pieces.

Step-by-step examples like these are an excellent way to convey your organizational, problem-solving, and conceptual abilities.

Designing Graphics

Creating a graphic system is your next step. You accomplish this by deciding how you're going to mount your artwork and photos, and by choosing which typefaces you'll use for your resume, captions, and subject dividers. These decisions, in turn, determine (or limit) your choice of binders or containers, and of colors for the matboard and paper you'll use for mounting. If you keep your graphic system as simple as possible (unless you've had a lot of graphic design experience) you'll be happier with the results.

After you've made a rough list of how you want the artwork and verbal information in your portfolio organized, you can begin to make the above-mentioned design decisions.

Step 6: Constructing Your Portfolio

Now that you have a plan for your portfolio, you must convert those pieces of your artwork that are larger than the physical dimensions of the portfolio you've selected.

You'll have to photograph them and get prints to fit your portfolio's dimensions. Since it takes about two weeks to shoot slides, have them processed, edit them, order prints from the best slides, and receive the finished enlargements, it's a good idea to photograph your art first and work then on your graphics, your resume, captions and other verbal information while your film and prints are being processed. (See the appendices for advice on photographing artwork.)

Construction Supplies

While you are waiting for your prints, you can buy your graphics materials, art paper, mat board, binder, page protectors and any tools you'll need to construct and assemble your portfolio.

You'll probably need an x-acto knife and blades, a good steel ruler, rubdown lettering, spray fixative to protect the lettering, spray adhesive, a good, long, and accurate T-square, a straight 12" triangle, and a drawing board with a square edge for the T-square to slide

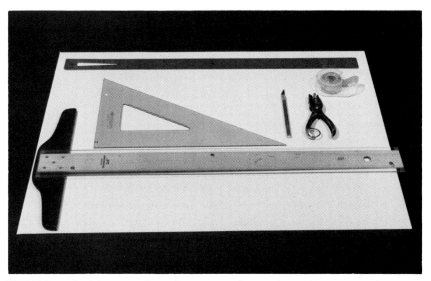

FIGURE 5. Good basic graphic tools are essential to good portfolio craftsmanship. A T-square, triangle, X-acto knife, hole punch, masking tape, and ruler are invaluable.

against. In addition, you'll need drafting or masking tape, rubber cement, and Bestine (rubber cement thinner) for cleaning your tools, for removing overspray from the spray glue, and for removing cemented pieces of artwork from their backings if they are positioned incorrectly.

If the binder you select is ringed, you will certainly need a standard, inexpensive ¼" hole punch. If you're typing your captions, resume and cover letter and your typewriter ribbon isn't very black anymore, buy a new ribbon.

If your portfolio is well thought out before you buy your art supplies, you will have a good idea of how much art paper, mat board, rubdown lettering, and slide and page protectors you will need. Make a list of what you will need, then add a few of each item to your shopping list so that you will have some extra supplies in case you make changes, a mistake, or decide to add more to your portfolio later. Even if your plan isn't thought out page-by-page, write out a list of supplies you expect to use, and then add a few more of everything. Buying more art supplies than you actually need may cost more initially, but it will save you frustrating trips to the art supply store later on.

A final word of advice on purchasing your supplies: Buy good quality materials and tools. A wooden yardstick can't give you as straight a line or as accurate a measure as a good T-square, triangle, and etched stainless-steel ruler; and don't substitute cheap construction paper for good art paper. Also, don't let high prices alone influence your decisions about quality; don't assume that expensive means good. If one brand of rubdown type costs $5.00 a sheet and another brand is only $1.20 a sheet, find out which one will last longer. And since prices can vary significantly between art supply stores, shop for what you need, but never buy inferior products to save a little money.

The time, talent, and effort spent preparing your portfolio becomes even more worthwhile when you use quality materials.

How to Begin Construction

Once you have photographed your artwork, assembled all the materials and tools needed, and written a rough plan and then a page-by-page dummy, the next step is to put it all together.

Graphic designers and others who have experience working with graphic tools and materials can start right in on the graphic system, cutting and putting type down on subject dividers, mounting original artwork, and arranging photostats. The work should move quickly if you've designed the portfolio's elements properly.

Other designers and artists not as familiar with graphic tools and techniques should start slowly and deliberately on the simplest kind of work. If you feel most comfortable cutting paper and punching holes, do that work first and gradually move into the more difficult tasks, such as rubbing down type, applying zip film, or spray mounting a large photo.

All graphics work requires patience and attention to detail. Since good craftsmanship is so important to a successful portfolio, take all the time you need to do a good job. If you aren't sure about the proper way to use some material, experiment on a scrap first and look at the results. If it works, try it using the real artwork. Practice each new step that you don't feel comfortable with before applying it to the portfolio's construction.

If you find yourself getting angry or frustrated because you've made a mistake, leave everything as it is and walk away for a while, or go onto something easier. Graphics materials and artwork are fragile and don't usually survive bursts of temper. Your portfolio must be constructed slowly and meticulously.

Here are a few suggestions to improve your graphics craftsmanship:

- Clean your work area and tools thoroughly before you begin work each day.
- Do all of your spraying in a well-ventilated area away from your cutting or drawing area.
- Spread out lots of paper around your spraying area and spray each piece of paper or artwork on a fresh page of newspaper, turning the page after each spray.
- Work in a well-lit area.
- Wash your hands well before starting work and wash them frequently as you work. Sweat and oils that accumulate on your hands can stain and damage papers, photos, and graphic materials very easily.
- Dry your hands thoroughly, as well. Moisture leaves permanent stains.
- Most importantly, though, take enough time to do the kind of work your portfolio deserves.

For instructions on how to use specific materials, see Chapter 4.

3.
Two Examples: Portfolios for a Graphic Designer and an Artist

ORGANIZING A GRAPHIC DESIGNER'S PORTFOLIO

Let's say that you are a graphic designer and you want to find a better job. You've been out of school for a year or two. Let's also assume that you've given yourself about three weeks to put together a portfolio, and hope to find a new job in about two months. This schedule should allow you plenty of time to properly assemble the portfolio and to carefully examine employment opportunities. It's never good to be in a financial position where you must get a job immediately, since it prevents you from taking the time to carefully consider all of your employment options. Three weeks should be enough time to put together this portfolio.

Your list of tasks should read as follows:
- Gather artwork
- Evaluate artwork
- Select artwork
- Photograph oversize or work in use
- Evaluate presentation process
- Select portfolio format
- Design portfolio
- Assemble portfolio

Assemble the Artwork

Gather as many samples of your work as you can. The better their condition, the better they'll look in the portfolio. Printed pieces should be flat or properly folded. The print quality should be high, in good register and trimmed to actual finish size. Comprehensive layouts, finished presentation or concept sketches can represent work that was never actually printed.

Evaluate the Artwork

Spread the work on a table and remove samples of the work you do not want to show, either because it represents the kind of work you

FIGURE 6. This designer has organized the work he wants to show into stacks. Posters are on the left; announcements and catalogs are in the center; and identity program pieces are to the right. He will maintain this kind of organization in the finished portfolio.

don't want to do, or because the quality of the work is inferior.

Then evaluate the remaining samples. Sort them according to use or graphic technique. Put identity design samples together. Separate advertisements from announcements, brochures, or fliers. Group larger pieces like posters or charts separately. Then evaluate each category for its strengths and weaknesses. Edit them further so that the work remaining is representative of your best skills and experience.

Photograph Oversize Samples and Some of Your Designs in Use

Not all graphic design is small in size. Many designers plan and produce signage programs, displays, maps and charts, and environmental graphics. Examples of work of this scale should be photographed. Do it yourself properly or hire someone to do it for you. Don't depend on Polaroids or snapshots to professionally convey the work.

You might also think of ways to imaginatively illustrate your work in use. Say that you've designed a logo that's used for a retail store in many different ways. A photograph of your logo on the storefront window might be more impressive than a black-and-white photostat of the same design. If your logo has been used on shopping bags, photograph someone walking out of the store carrying one of the bags filled with merchandise. A little thought given to showing your designs in use will add interest to your entire portfolio.

Evaluate the Presentation Process

If you will be interviewing with your work, you will need a portfolio that is easily portable, and easy to speak from. A toothed binder or individual boards will probably suit your needs best.

If you're mailing a portfolio, a smaller version would be more practical. A simple thin notebook is appropriate for a slide portfolio that will be mailed.

Let's assume that you will be interviewing with your work and you think a toothed binder would work best for you. Since most initial interviews last about half an hour, select enough artwork to take up about 15 minutes of that time. Select the work from the categories you chose.

Next, consider the size of your portfolio. If most of your pieces are small format, select a small binder. If much of your work is poster size, you may want to photograph the work and use a small binder for the photos, or you may want to fold the oversize pieces to fit.

A good way to choose a format for medium sized work is to select the average size piece and design each page a little larger than that. For example, if you have a magazine ad that opens up to 11 x 17", a 12 x 18"

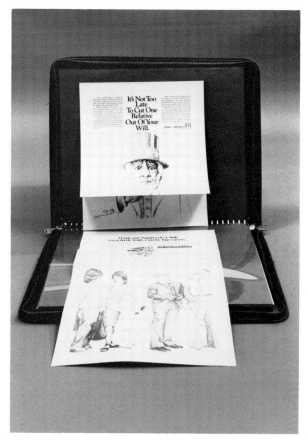

FIGURE 7. *Dugald Stermer's work has been folded to fit into this portfolio. These two sheets were longer than most of the other work shown, so rather than make the entire portfolio format large enough to accommodate these pieces, they were folded instead. Poster size samples are carried in a drawing tube and are shown after the presentation is made with the binder.*

portfolio page comfortably accommodates it. Let that be your binder page size. Work larger than the page size can be folded to fit. (See photo)

Design Your Portfolio

With the work you want and the size selected, you can design the portfolio. You can decide the order of the pieces, the color of the backing sheets, the kind of verbal information you need to support the samples, and the page format. An outline of the contents of the portfolio is a good first step to designing the portfolio.

I.   Front matter
       Title divider—grey mat board
       Resume

Photograph of designer
Copy of any self-promotion pieces
II.   Advertising graphics
4   full color ad spreads
5   black-and-white ads
Newspaper ads
III. Corporate identity
Logos, letterheads
Sequential annual report information
Photos of final projects, store identity
IV.   Slides of work not included in printed samples
V.   Loose samples

As a graphic designer, you should have an idea of how the whole package will look. A grid layout for positioning samples might be appropriate if your work lends itself to that kind of organization.

You should select a design which accentuates your work. Any press down type or captions should be impeccably handled. If you're comfortable working with some of the many new presentation materials, like color comping processes, it might be worthwhile to consider using them.

As a graphic designer, too, you have a choice whether you want your portfolio to be a graphic tour de force, or an understated binder that lets the samples alone represent your work. Whichever you decide, and there are many reasons to recommend each style, be consistent in your approach and the result will be more successful.

Assemble Your Portfolio

With the organization and design complete, you can assemble the actual portfolio. Chapters 4 and 5 are full of helpful techniques you may want to use.

ORGANIZING A FINE ARTIST'S PORTFOLIO

If you're a fine artist putting together a portfolio of artwork to show to galleries, art consultants or agents, you're not looking for a job, but representation. You want to show only your work and not your employment history.

Your list of steps should read as follows:
• Gather artwork or photos of artwork
• Evaluate and select examples

- Photograph or re-photograph the work
- Evaluate the presentation process
- Select the portfolio format
- Design the portfolio
- Assemble the portfolio

Gather Artwork

While the graphic designer can get several copies of a printed piece for a portfolio, the fine artist usually works on original one-of-a-kind pieces. Much of an artist's work is sold or traded so the artist often doesn't even own the better work any more. If this is your problem, make a list of the better pieces and where they are, and then make arrangements to have them photographed.

Evaluate the Artwork

Look at your work and try to maintain objectivity to decide which pieces are the strongest, best executed, and representative of your long term artistic goals. Remove pieces that you think are inferior.

Next, compare older work with your most recent. Consider using the older work to show a long term development and commitment to your ideas and skill. Your portfolio should emphasize recent work, since it is the work a gallery would be most interested in selling. Select about 10 to 15 of your very best pieces. Never include inferior work. For a fine artist, one genuinely bad piece really can spoil the work shown with it in the same portfolio. While a designer works to please a client, an artist works to please himself; and the artist has no one else to blame if a piece is bad.

Photograph the Artwork

With the best pieces selected, photograph them. If you're going to be showing color prints of the work, be sure to get good color reproduction. Prints should be large enough to show the details of the work.

If you are photographing your own work, take the time to study how to do it properly. (See Appendix and the Bibliography) If you aren't able to photograph the work, hire someone to do it for you. There are photographers who specialize in artwork photography. Local galleries or professional photo labs can tell you who they are.

Good photography is usually expensive, but a good, sharp, accurate photograph looks so much more professional than a bleary Polaroid or snapshot. Serious artists understand the importance of good slides and photographs and either learn to do it the correct way, or pay the pros to do it for them.

Evaluate the Presentation Process

If you are approaching galleries in person, you will be in an interview situation and should design the portfolio to speak from. Prints and slides are appropriate, supported by announcements of previous shows, reviews, catalogs that include your work, and a list of exhibitions.

A somewhat reduced portfolio can be assembled for mailing: a set of slides, some show announcements, and a list of exhibitions, all bound in a thin notebook. Include a return envelope, addressed and stamped.

Select a Portfolio Format

If your portfolio is in photographic form, a three ring binder is probably the best way to organize it. Using slide pages and page sleeves, the photos will be protected and easy to see. If you're showing original work, though, you will have to decide which way will give your work the most protection. Photos of examples of individual portfolios are shown through the rest of the book.

Design the Portfolio

For the fine artist, the design of a standard portfolio should be a simple matter of selecting a binder, slide pages and page sleeves, and grouping the photos in a logical progression. For an artist making a custom portfolio, the task is more complicated. Whether you're making a print box portfolio, a jewelry box, a hand-stitched carrying case, or a fabricated steel photo vault, the craftsmanship must be superb if it is going to make its impact the way you want it to.

Assemble the Portfolio

After you have decided how to design your portfolio, you can put it all together. Organize your photographs or slides. Caption them. Put your exhibition list, photograph of you (if you are going to use one), and the clippings and reviews together neatly and carefully.

4.
Binders, Materials, Graphic Products and Services—and How to Use Them

The physical characteristics of your portfolio—its size, binder, page covers, colors, and graphic products—can make as much of a statement about your abilities as the art you carry within it. This chapter will introduce you to the many materials available for portfolio construction.

BINDERS

Three-Ring Notebooks — You can make a good portfolio quickly and inexpensively using an 8½ x 11" three-ring binder. There are many accessories available to fit a three-ring format, such as vinyl page protectors designed to hold 8½ x 11" sheets, and they can be found in many stationery, camera, and art supply stores.

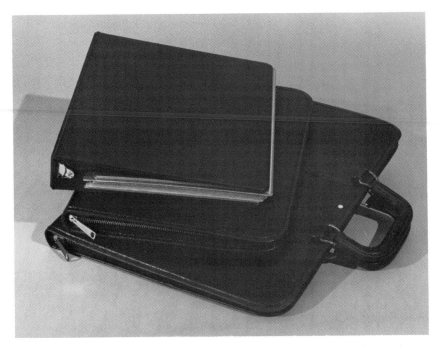

FIGURE 8. *Each of these kinds of binders can make suitable portfolios. The top one is a three-ring binder for 8½ x 11" artwork. The middle one is also a three-ring binder, but it zips closed on all sides. The bottom binder is toothed and easily accommodates artwork up to 11 x 14". The bottom portfolio is available in sizes up to 18 x 24", and even larger than that without the rings.*

Three-ring binders have a number of advantages. They're durable, inexpensive, easy to handle, and small enough to be shipped cheaply and safely. It's also easy to design for them.

Their one real disadvantage is that artwork larger than 8½ x 11" has to be reduced to fit the binder. If your artwork is very large and you have to photograph it to make it small enough for *any* sized binder, then you may as well select the more convenient 8½ x 11" format. If your work is small, but not that small, choose a binder large enough to hold the original artwork.

Toothed Binders — Toothed binders are available in several sizes, from 11 x 14" to 18 x 24". The larger sizes aren't practical for portfolios that must be taken to interviews because their size makes them awkward to handle and heavy to carry; and it's difficult to display small pieces of art in them. An 18 x 24" toothed binder unfolds to take up over six square feet of desktop space, making smaller formats much more sensible for standard professional portfolios.

But even the smaller toothed binders are not without problems. The

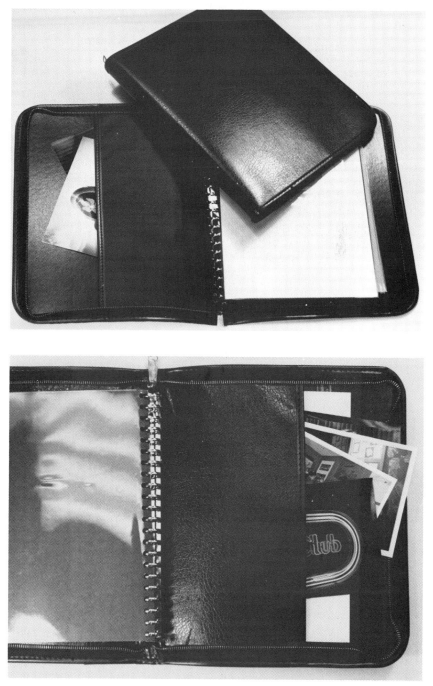

FIGURES 9-10. These toothed binders have full zippers to close them completely and pockets on the insides of the covers to hold loose photos, extra resumes, or samples of artwork that you don't mind an interviewer handling.

FIGURE 11. *Unfortunately, acetate sleeves sold with toothed binders rip out and tear and should be replaced. Vinyl page protectors aren't available for toothed binders.*

ones available in most stores are poorly designed and not as flexible or adaptable as three-ring binders. Perhaps the most irritating design feature of the toothed binder is the excessive number of rings used to hold the pages in place. In the 11 x 14″ binder, twenty-eight rings are used where five or six would suffice. Each time a page is turned, at least one hole snags on a ring and has to be disentagled by hand; so turning the pages of a toothed binder during a quick portfolio presentation can become an awkward and frustrating experience.

Another drawback is that the accessories made for toothed binders are limited to thin acetate sleeves, usually sold with the binder. Slide-protector-format sleeves aren't available for toothed binders, and the acetate sleeves have some major problems: they're not durable, often ripping around ring holes and cracking along outside edges; they reflect a lot of light, so that the viewer finds himself trying to see your artwork *in spite* of the page protectors; and they attract dust and dirt, which can lead to scratched and dull-looking pages if your portfolio is frequently used. The vinyl page protectors available for three-ring binders eliminate many of these problems, but they're not made to fit toothed binders.

Still, toothed binders themselves are well made of fine, sturdy materials and hardware, and they come in a good selection of sizes. They are, in fact, the binders that most designers own and use.

FIGURE 12. The ring arrangement for an 8½ x 11" slide page can be repunched to fit a toothed binder using a template and ¼" hole punch.

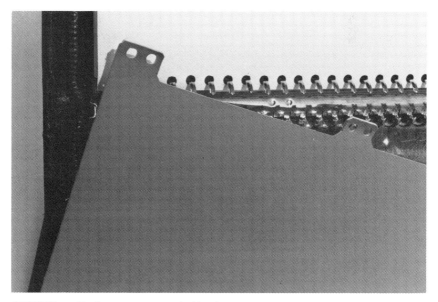

FIGURE 13. By designing your toothed binder inserts so as to bypass most of the holes in the binder, you can use only as many rings as are necessary to hold the artwork into place.

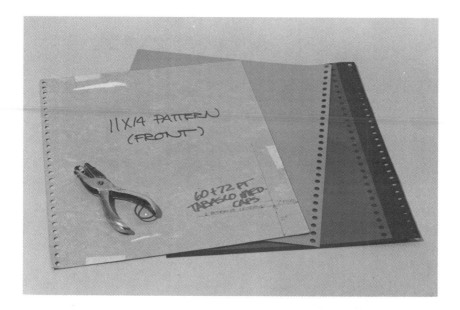

FIGURES 14-15. *Divider templates constructed of a heavy stock or railroad board make fitting work to your portfolio much easier.*

The acetate sleeves, or page protectors, can be modified so as not to frequently snag on the rings. One way is to enlarge each hole slightly with a hole punch. Another method is to cut them so that you are only using a few of the holes (and rings) to keep the pages in place. Still another alternative is to make the sleeves into single slip sheets by cutting the fold in the acetate with an x-acto knife; this will leave you with two sheets of acetate instead of one per sleeve, which will reduce snags.

Whether you are using all of the rings or not, you will need a template cut out of thin cardboard, the same size as your portfolio pages. Punch the hole pattern, just as it is on a page protector along the left-hand edge of the template. Use this template to convert smaller three-ring slide protectors, mat board subject dividers, sheets of art paper, and artwork to fit onto your toothed portfolio rings.

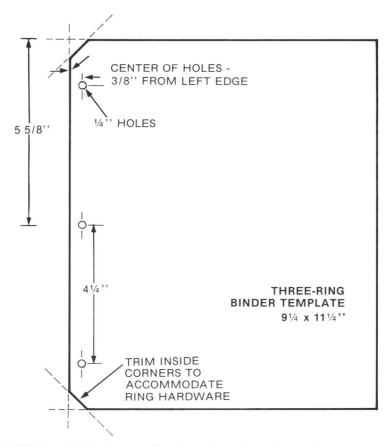

CENTER OF HOLES - 3/8'' FROM LEFT EDGE

¼'' HOLES

5 5/8''

4¼''

THREE-RING
BINDER TEMPLATE
9¼ x 11¼''

TRIM INSIDE
CORNERS TO
ACCOMMODATE
RING HARDWARE

FIGURE 16. Make a heavy cardboard template as shown above and use it for a cutting and hole punching pattern. Cut art paper, mat board, photostats, printed samples, or anything you want to insert in your binder. 9¼ x 11¼" is the size of three-hole slide and page protectors.

Slide Portfolios — Slide portfolios are usually very small and can be assembled quickly with a few three-ring, 8½ x 11" slide protectors and a page protector for your resume. Put them in a snap binder instead of a ring binder, because snap binders are flatter and more easily mailed. Also, the snaps pull apart easily, which encourages the viewer to take slide pages out of the binder to look at them more carefully.

As will be explained more fully in the section in Chapter 8 on labeling and filing slides, you can find an appropriate slide-identification system to use in your portfolio. Such a system will make your slide portfolio easier to view than the same slides, loose and poorly marked, in a box.

Accessories — Because of the odd physics of any type of ring binder, the first and last pages in such a binder are frequently pinched between the rings and the binder cover. Various attempts have been made by binder manufacturers to remedy this problem. Some companies have tried to prevent this by altering the shape of the ring itself. Others have moved the position of the rings. A more common solution is to use plastic strip shields at the front and back of your three-ring binder. If the binder you buy doesn't have strip shields, you can buy them as separate items in stationery stores.

In any bound portfolio, the very first sheet is the one subjected to the most wear; so it's a good idea to create the first page out of a durable material like polyester film, perhaps a film positive with a design or your name photostated into place. (See the process-camera services section of

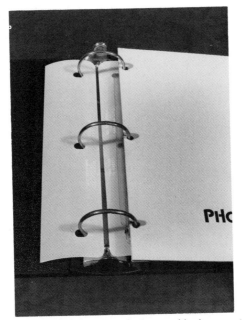

FIGURE 17. Plastic strip shields help protect the front and back pages of a three-ring binder.

this chapter.)

Polyester film is much stronger than acetate and will not rip out at the holes. In fact, the way to distinguish between acetate and polyester films is to try to tear them. Acetate rips easily while polyester won't rip at all.

Another possible solution is to use heavy plastic punched to fit your binder rings. Plastic supply houses carry large sheets of thin polyester or vinyl that are strong enough to endure the wear that the first page will get.

Mat board isn't really a satisfactory material for a first page because it becomes dogeared and stained unless it's protected by a transparent sheet of film, or replaced frequently.

Plexiglas, which comes as thin as 1/16th of an inch—colored, tinted, or clear—can look especially slick in your binder, either as a first page or as a subject divider. However, with Plexiglas you should drill the holes rather than punch them. It's a beautiful material when properly used, but it scratches very easily. You can't expect clear Plexiglas to look like crystal for very long. Smokey, translucent, or colored Plexiglas will probably look less scratched after moderate use than the clear. Plexiglas can also be sanded to look like etched glass.

Since it's such an inflexible material, drill the holes slightly larger than you would punch them for a more flexible material: ⅜" holes would be better than ¼" holes since they wouldn't catch and snag as easily as you turn the pages of your portfolio.

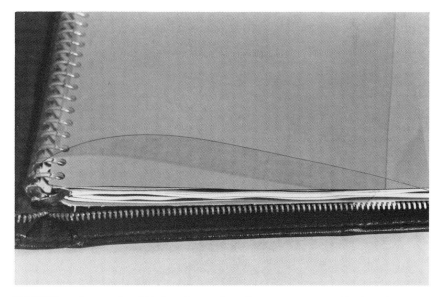

FIGURE 18. In any ringed binder, the very first sheet wears more quickly than the interior pages. A single piece of polyester film or thick vinyl, cut and punched to fit the ring arrangement, will keep your first page looking fresh and neat for much longer.

FIGURE 19. *Vinyl three-ring page and slide protectors come in a variety of sizes. Here are four types: the top sheets protect 2¼ x 2¼" transparencies; the second is 8 x 10"; the third is a slide page for 35mm transparencies; and the bottom sheet protects 8½ x 11" pages.*

FIGURE 20. *This three-ring binder didn't have a built-in pouch for loose photos, business cards, extra resumes, and clippings, so the designer cut the top third off of a vinyl page protector and put it in at the end of his portfolio.*

Cases for Loose Artwork — For loose artwork, several styles of carrying cases are available. Most have handles and sturdy zippers. The most popular models are made of canvas or simulated leather. They are similar in appearance to the toothed binders, but since they don't have any binding hardware inside, these artwork cases are considerably less expensive.

Durable tubes with handles are made to carry drafting samples or rolls of drawings. They come in several lengths.

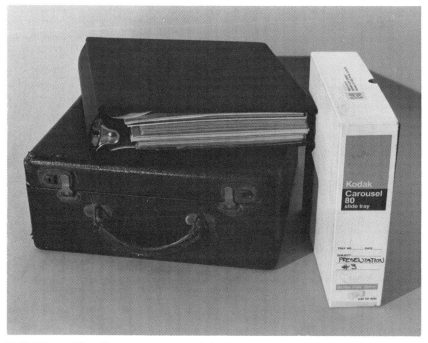

FIGURE 21. This old typewriter case easily holds a thick three-ring portfolio and a carousel slide tray. Besides being a sturdy piece of luggage that can take the wear of traveling, this case is old enough to add a little charm and interest to the entire portfolio package.

Permanent Bindings

There are a few ways to permanently bind your portfolio if you know you won't be adding more artwork to it. Permanent binding is especially useful for documentary portfolios because they describe already completed projects to which nothing can be added.

Perhaps the most handsome way to permanently bind a portfolio is with a spiral binding. A spiral-bound book needs about a ½" margin on the bound side of the pages so that there is room for the holes that the spiral wire passes through. All of the pages, collated into proper order and positioned correctly, are drilled at the same time. Then, a wire is threaded through the holes in loops up the side of your book. The result is a simply and attractively bound portfolio with pages that will open flat and turn easily.

There are some restrictions to this method of binding. The thickness of your book should be limited to one inch or less; the book's dimensions should be kept small—8½ x 11″ is a good size—and all of your pages should be of uniform-size paper or mat board.

If the idea of a spiral-bound portfolio appeals to you, you'll have to locate a source that can do the work. Spiral binding is usually available in large cities, but rarely in smaller towns. Since spiral binding may be more expensive than you can afford, get a quote from the company before you order the work done. Also, deliver your portfolio to the spiral-binding company in person so that you can make sure your instructions are understood. If you can't locate a spiral-binding company in your area, try to get the name of one from any printing company nearby.

FIGURE 22. Permanent binding may be appropriate for special or documentary portfolios. Commonly available methods include velo binding, top; spiral binding; or comb, or GBC binding. Books on hand bookbinding are listed in the Bibliography.

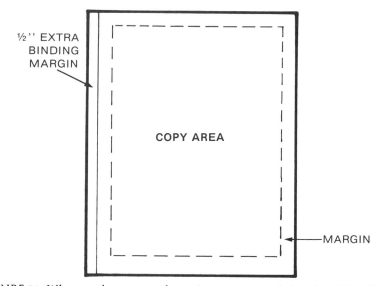

FIGURE 23. When you plan your page layout for any permanently bound portfolio, allow at least ½" extra margin on the binding edge so that the binding doesn't interfere with the copy area.

A less expensive form of permanent binding is Velo binding, which consists of a thin strip of plastic with straight posts running through the sheets of paper. However, a portfolio bound this way will not open to lie flat. Velo binding works best for small printed reports or catalogs.

Binding services are sometimes listed in the Yellow Pages of the phone book under *Covers—Book, Catalog.*

PORTFOLIO MATERIALS

The following list should encourage you to consider using unfamiliar materials in your portfolio. It's a partial list, of course, but the materials presented can help you create more interesting ways to display your work. The advantages and disadvantages of each material are also explained.

Acetate — Acetate page protectors are provided with most toothed binders. They are available for three-ring binders as well, and usually come with grey-black construction paper sandwiched between the sheets. Acetate is a brittle plastic that rips easily and, when rattled, makes a tinny noise. When possible, use either polyester or vinyl page protectors instead.

Polyester — It's a stronger, more durable plastic than acetate. Film positives made with polyester film are strong enough to be punched and inserted directly into the portfolio and will not rip out. They can also be used as first sheets in any kind of binder and will take lots of wear. Polyester is dimensionally stable and won't shrink or expand in heat.

Vinyl — Vinyl is a flexible and durable plastic, more rubbery than the three other plastics described. It's easily formed with heat, which is why many products are made from it. Slide pages, page protectors, and large clear envelopes are available in vinyl. Several large mail-order outfits manufacture entire lines of portfolio products, most of which are made from vinyl. Vinyl is not dimensionally stable, so it will shrink around photos and pages if left in the heat of a parked car or in direct sunlight, and will become brittle in the cold.

Plexiglas — Plexiglas is a relatively inflexible material available in translucent tints, and in transparent and colored sheets of many thicknesses. It is easily scratched, and will be expensive if you buy a lot of it. When used in a binder, Plexiglas shouldn't be any thicker than ⅛". It can be drilled, sawed, buffed, polished, glued, laminated, and inlayed if you have good tools and handle it carefully. Plexiglas can give a portfolio a very finished look that can't be duplicated with other materials when handled properly; but proper handling requires skill and experience. Design mistakes in Plexiglas can be costly, so be careful and patient when you use it.

If you've decided to use Plexiglas in your portfolio, make a cardboard mock-up done to exactly the page size you want. Drill the holes and glue the seams just as you want them on the actual page. Check the design details carefully to be sure you have what you want. Then take this mock-up to the Plexiglas sales person. If you are doing the work yourself, he may be able to sell you scraps and waste pieces for less than a whole sheet. If you are having a plastic craftsman do the work, this mock-up will guarantee that you'll end up with what you want.

Fabrics — If your work involves fabrics—weaving, costume, fashion, or textile design—then it's appropriate to use fabrics in your portfolio. Cloth-covered binders can add color and texture to your portfolio, but only if you're good at tailoring corners and edges and at folding joints. Thin cloths make better portfolio covers than heavy woven fabrics.

If you aren't good at tight tailoring you could end up with a raggedy portfolio, so you should stick to a regular binder and make a cloth carrying case for it, perhaps with pockets for loose samples and business cards. Heavier weaves of cloth can very quickly be fashioned into bags to which you can attach a shoulder strap or carrying handles. Quilted, dyed, stitched, or appliqued binder cases can exhibit those of your skills

FIGURE 24. This detail of Taj Diffenbaugh Worley's print and paper portfolio shows the artist's fine tailoring ability.

that might go unappreciated if you tried to show them in photographs.

Unless you are a textile designer, it's not usually a good idea to put too many fabric samples inside the actual portfolio. If you have page after page of pieces of cloth, it can start to look like a swatch book.

Mat Board — Mat board comes in a wide range of colors. It can be used for subject dividers, and as backing for photographs, artwork, and storyboards.

Mat board usually has one finished side and one unfinished side. The unfinished side should be covered with art paper wherever it will be exposed during a presentation. To do this, spray the back of the board and the back of the paper with glue, lay the paper over the board (sticky surfaces together), and roll or burnish the paper to the board for a strong bond. If you laminate whole sheets of mat board and paper and then cut pieces to size, your edges will be sharper and cleaner than if you do the lamination after the board is cut.

To cut mat board, you'll need a very sharp mat or x-acto knife and a steel straightedge or ruler. Mark the board for cutting with light lines, using a soft pencil to facilitate easy erasing. Always cut mat board on a soft surface, like another sheet of board, because it makes cutting easier and keeps your knife sharp longer. Also, be sure to wash your hands before working with colored mat board—it stains very easily.

FIGURES 25-29. *Using a template to cut mat board for section dividers is a simple procedure.*

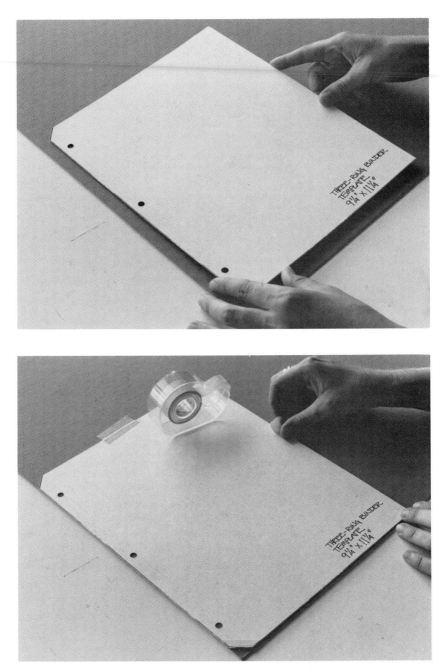

FIGURES 25-26. *Place template over the mat board and tape it into position.*

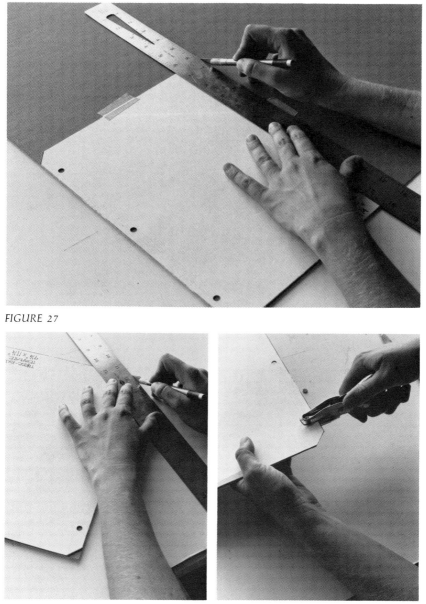

FIGURE 27

FIGURE 28   FIGURE 29

FIGURES 27-28. Cut the matboard with a mat or X-acto knife, using a steel ruler or straightedge as a cutting edge.

FIGURE 29. Punch the mat board where indicated on the template with a ¼" hole punch.

FIGURES 30-35. Mat board used as a sectional divider looks better if it's backed with art paper. This procedure is also simple.

FIGURE 30. Cut art paper larger than the mat board divider.

FIGURE 31

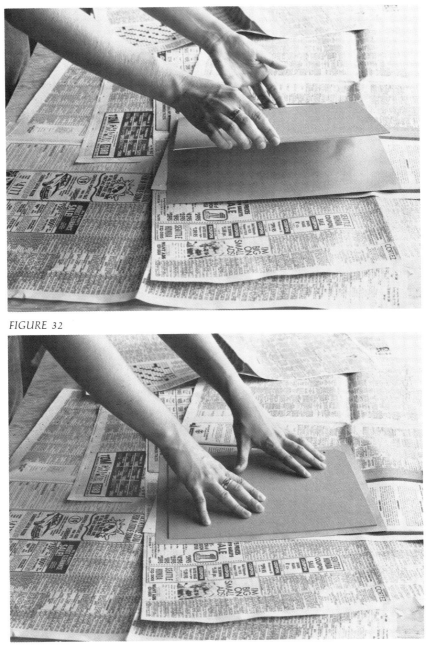

FIGURE 32

FIGURE 33

FIGURES 31-33. Using spray adhesive, glue facing sides of the mat board and art paper and press them together, leaving a border of art paper all around the divider.

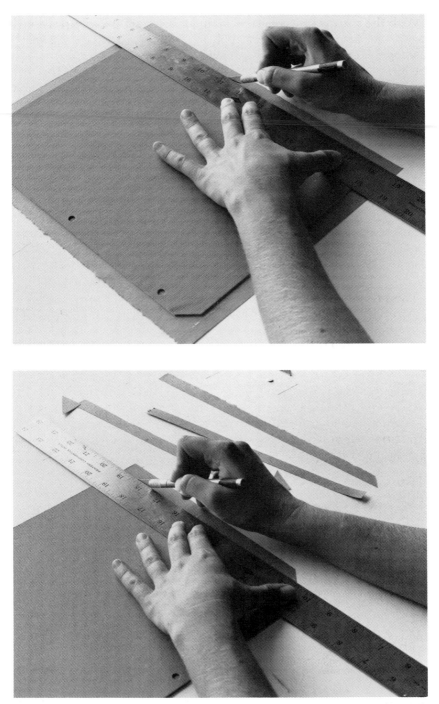

FIGURES 34-35. Trim off the excess art paper, again using a steel straightedge as the cutting edge. Then punch the holes.

With the cutting lines penciled in, hold the straightedge firmly on the board—the more pressure you apply as you cut, the less chance there is of irregular edges—and make a shallow cut, holding the knife parallel to the board. With the blade angled so that its tip is cutting into the board, make another cut in the same place, this time using more pressure. Holding your straightedge in place, continue cutting along the same line until you have cut through the mat board completely.

If your straightedge slips slightly while you are cutting, creating a dip on the board's edge, make a new cutting line a hair past the dip and start again. That way your edge will be much cleaner than if you tried to even out the dip. If your edges look good and sharp but have a few burrs on them, sand them off with fine sandpaper; don't pick or pull at the burrs.

Plastic Lamination — One excellent way to protect flat pieces of printed artwork, such as posters, postcards, brochures, flyers, singles sheets of stationery, or even magazine articles, is to have them laminated in clear plastic. It's a specialty process that involves sandwiching the paper between clear vinyl sheets.

This process isn't appropriate for one-of-a-kind drawings paintings, or illustrations, but it is great for printed samples or photostats of artwork.

Once you locate a source for lamination, ask about their services, explain what you would like, and ask for their suggestions. The thickness of plastic can vary. Five mil plastic gives you a durable surface that can still be rolled up. Perhaps you would like a stiffer plastic, or an opaque plastic backing. Folded pieces can be laminated, but there are usually problems with complex folds because of the extra thickness of the plastic and the edges the plastic creates. If you aren't sure about the suitability of lamination for your portfolio, try a piece or two, check the results, and then decide if it's a good way for you to protect your work.

FIGURE 36. This detail photo shows plastic lamination of printed pieces. Lamination protects the paper surface by sealing the printed piece between two sheets of 5 mil clear plastic. This process is an excellent way to protect graphic design or illustration samples, clippings, or tear sheets from magazines or newspapers.

Art Papers — Art papers are sold in art supply stores, and they come in many beautiful colors. They are several grades better than inexpensive construction paper. Sold by the sheet, in sizes ranging from 20 x 24" to 30 x 40", art papers can be used in many ways in your portfolio. One of art paper's excellent features is that while it's generally lightweight enough not to add a lot of bulk to your portfolio, it's also heavy enough to take spray glues, rubber cement, and tape without wrinkling.

In toothed binders, the grey-black paper provided with the sleeve protectors should be replaced with an interesting colored paper or with a richer, darker black. If you're using vinyl page protectors, you can mount the work you're showing in 8½ x 11" pieces of art paper whose colors will accentuate your artwork.

When selecting colors, remember that subtle hues usually help the work while bright and garish ones compete with it. Also, keep the colors compatible with one another since they'll be bound in the same portfolio. The colors you select can help to tie a lot of diverse work into a consistent whole.

FIGURE 37. *If you plan to use both sides of a page to display artwork, mount each piece on a separate sheet of paper so that you can shuffle the organization of your portfolio without disturbing artwork that will remain in place.*

Occasionally, you can find an art supply store that sells a company's entire paper line, with mat board and art paper coming in the same colors. This might be helpful, especially if you want exactly the same shades of color throughout your portfolio.

When you buy paper, check to see if one side is the same color as the other. If the shades are subtly yet noticeably different, remember to work on the same sides of the paper while you are assembling the portfolio.

Heavy art paper makes better section dividers in small ring or toothed binders than mat board, which is too thick and takes up too much space on the rings.

You can type on art paper with a standard typewriter, which will give you better looking captions. If your typewriter has pressure settings, use more pressure on art paper than you would on regular bond typing paper.

Printing Paper — Printing papers come in a terrific range of colors, textures, and weights. But since most printing is done on lighter, thinner paper, the selection of colors and weight a small print shop might carry is limited. Larger printing companies (and certainly the paper companies themselves) stock some very beautiful colors. In fact, Strathmore sells their color paper as both art and printing stock. If you buy your paper from a print shop, though, it should cost you less than in an art supply store. Printing papers are always cheaper than art papers, but you usually have to buy them in quantities rather than by the sheet.

Metals — In some circumstances, metal or metalic materials can greatly enhance your portfolio, especially if the work you're showing relates to metal sculpture, craft, or design. A stainless steel binder, specially fabricated for you, could be an extra impressive and very expensive touch that would make your portfolio stand out in an interviewer's mind.

If you work with metal and want to bring it into your portfolio without spending money on a custom-made metal item, consider using some of the available metalic papers or mylar sheets instead; they can convey the impression of metal without its expense or fabrication difficulties. Of course, metalic papers aren't as durable as real metal, so you'll have to protect their surfaces (inside the portfolio) from scratches with tissue slip sheets. If you are considering metalic papers for your portfolio, try a test sheet first before buying all you will need. It may not work at all well for the purposes you had in mind.

Some of the buffed metal surfaces that have a brushed texture can take rubdown type fairly well; as long as the surface isn't handled, the type should stay in place. Also available are the vinyl letters used for outdoor signs (and sold by the same companies that make rubdown type); they can be used to make very durable and handsome letters and words, but are made only in a few type styles.

Leather and Wood — A well-crafted leather or wood binder or box portfolio can look strikingly handsome, but only if the workmanship of such a binder is superior; otherwise, the artist or designer should stay with a regular carrying case or binder. A leather or wood case has to stand up on its own as a piece of artwork and design.

Occasionally, you may run across an old leather case or wooden box in a junk or antique shop that is about the right size and proportion for a special portfolio or a storyboard presentation case. If you think your work would gain character by being presented in such a fine old musty carrying case, then buy it and convert all or part of your portfolio into this kind of format. Older cases and binders would be most appropriate for showing traditional forms of art or design, period or historical interiors, restoration architecture or design, traditional crafts, stylistically dated graphics, and old-school fine art. If you design art deco style graphics, an art deco style binder or carrying case could reinforce the impression you want your work to make.

GRAPHIC PRODUCTS

You will probably use graphic products like rubdown lettering, zip film, and transfer textures and symbols to create a graphic system for your portfolio. Unless you're a graphic artist familiar with these art aids, you will need to take some time to learn how to use them properly. Most of them require only a little manual dexterity and a lot of care for craftmanship, and, with practice, any artist or designer can use them.

Many of the companies that manufacture transfer type make entire lines of graphic products and advertise them in large, detailed catalogs. Frequently sold in art supply stores or available by mail, these catalogs are filled with information and instructions on how to use the products. You'll save time, money, and aggravation if you read these instructions before embarking on a buying spree of graphic products. The applications of some of these products are so broad that you'll probably want to experiment with a combination of them when you get a basic working knowledge of their possibilities. Conduct your experiments on scrap material before you try them on finished artwork; misplaced and inproperly removed transfer type can ruin a piece of artwork.

Transfer Lettering — Transfer lettering is a simple and direct way to add attractive type to your portfolio. Most rubdown type works the same way: a transparent piece of thin plastic, with alphabets of a single size

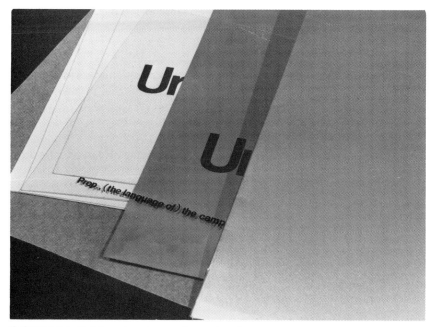

FIGURE 38. Rubdown lettering can be tranferred onto acetate, metallic paper, and brushed metal, as well as paper. Unusual surfaces do, however, require special care in letter application.

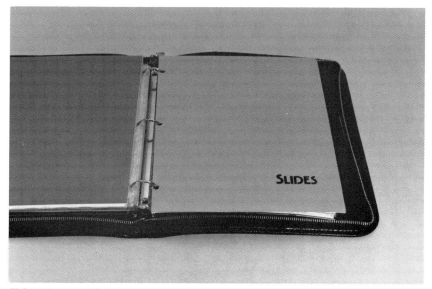

FIGURE 39. Rubdown transfer type on colored mat board provides a simple subject divider to separate sections of this three-ring zippered portfolio. A simple graphic system like this can be an effective way to unify an eclectic collection of work or assignments.

and type face, is positioned over the artwork to be lettered; the letter is burnished off of the carrier sheet and onto the artwork; and the carrier sheet is gently lifted, leaving the burnished letter on the artwork. By carefully rubbing a letter at a time, you can build consistently spaced words that are even along the bottom edge of a page or divider. A well-done transfer-lettering job will look as though it's been professionally printed.

The names of the larger transfer type companies are given in the Suppliers List. You may find that matching type sizes and styles is much simpler if you buy consistently from the same manufacturer. Use the brand that's easiest for you to buy or order and you'll be less likely to experience the frustration of discovering that your art supply store is out of it. That's a problem common among graphic designers.

Because there are thousands of these graphic products available, it's difficult for smaller art supply stores to maintain adequate supplies. If you live in a smaller city that doesn't have a fully stocked art supply store, order your materials through the nearest large art supply store or college bookstore, or by mail or phone. Large art supply stores are completely accustomed to taking phone orders and shipping the items COD. If you know what you need, and if you think it's important to the work you're doing, it's worth the trouble and the extra shipping charge to order by phone.

FIGURES 40-43. A sheet of rubdown lettering is positioned and the letter is gently transferred with a dull object such as a burnisher. The sheet is carefully pulled away and the finished line of type is burnished through tissue paper and then sprayed with protective coating.

FIGURE 40

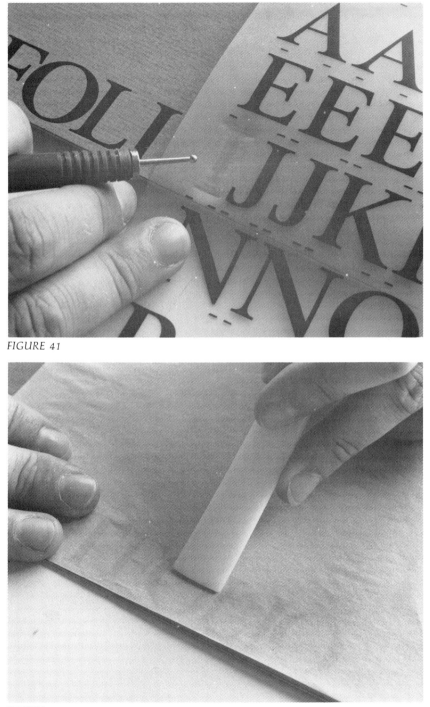

FIGURE 41

FIGURE 42

FIGURE 43

Some hints on using transfer type: First, make sure the surface you're applying the type to is clean and dry. Then, position the letter to be transferred in the exact spot you want it on the artwork, and, while holding the carrier sheet in one hand, lightly burnish the letter with smooth, even strokes, using an instrument with a broad, blunt point—transfer type manufacturers sell burnishers, but large, dull elementary school pencils work nicely, as well.

When the letter is completely transferred, it will look grey through the carrier sheet. Lift the sheet from the artwork slowly and, if the letter transferred properly, burnish it again, this time with the silicone sheet (that comes with the carrier sheet) on top of the letter to prevent it from scratching. The second burnishing makes the bond to the artwork more permanent and the type less fragile.

If the letter was misplaced, or if the wrong letter was transferred, it can be lifted off by gently dabbing it with masking tape. A letter that's hard to remove can be doused with Bestine (rubber cement thinner) and gently shaved off with a sharp x-acto knife blade. When the letter is completely removed, let the Bestine evaporate completely before trying to burnish another letter into place.

Perhaps the most difficult techniques to learn in transfer type are letter spacing and making lines of type straight and level. It takes practice and a careful eye to rub down a perfect line of type. Each of the type manufacturers incorporates its own spacing system into each sheet of type, which makes it easier for the novice. But to use transfer type properly, be sure that you understand the directions included in the manufacturer's catalog.

Custom Rubdowns --If you are unable to find appropriate type or symbols in standard transfer type catalogs, or if you would like rubdowns in a special color, it is possible to design and create custom rubdowns just the way you need them. Some of the major typesetting companies and photostat houses are offering this service. Although rather expensive it can add a lot of punch to your portfolio.

The process is simple. Order the type you need in the faces and sizes you want. Make any line art or symbols to size. Mount the type and line art onto a white board, select the colors you need, and send it off to the supplier. For economy you should try to group the elements as tightly as possible.

Some words of warning: get estimates first. Custom rubdowns are charged by size of the transfer sheets used and number of colors made. These costs add up quickly. Also, some suppliers are able to match a full range of Pantone colors, while others are only able to offer the standard primary and secondary colors. Discuss your requirements with your supplier first if you are uncertain about their requirements or capabilities.

FIGURE 44. These color rubdowns were custom made from type not available in transfer type catalogues. The type was set to size, mounted on art boards, and Pantone colors were specified. They transfer the same as commercial rubdowns.

FIGURE 44

Zip Films — Like rubdown lettering, zip film is a helpful graphic design product that's simple enough for non-graphic designers, artists, and architects to use effectively after only a little practice. Properly applied, zip film can greatly enhance a graphic project by adding uniform texture or color not easy to achieve using traditional drawing or painting techniques. The companies that manufacture zip color and texture are the same ones that make rubdown type, so both these products are usually available from the same art supply stores, or can be ordered through the same outlets.

   Rubdown texture is a similar product, but rather than cutting into the film and burnishing it onto the artwork, you position the sheet of texture over the artwork and rub down the texture directly in place.

FIGURE 45. Zip films are cut larger than necessary, positioned, and then trimmed to final size.

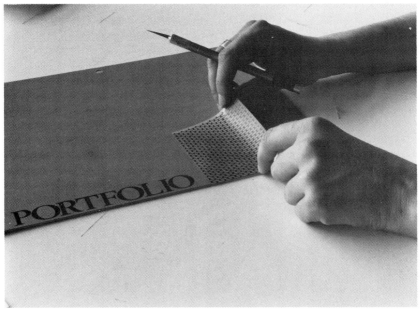

FIGURE 45

FIGURE 46.

Adhesives for Mounting Artwork and Photographs — Unless your photographs or artwork are the same size as your binder page or storyboard panel, you'll need to mount them onto a backing paper or mat board. It's difficult to remount photos or artwork once they're in place, so be sure you're putting them just where you want them before you glue them down.

For permanent mounts on paper, spray glue gives you a strong bond without the lumps and irregular thicknesses of rubber cement or paste. To glue with spray cement, position the trimmed photo or artwork onto the backing paper or board and, with a soft pencil, mark two or three corners of the work onto the backing paper. Then put the artwork face down onto a clean sheet of newspaper and spray a thin coat of glue over the back. Wait a few seconds, position the artwork using two of the marks on the mounting paper, and gently press. Wipe the artwork from the center to the edges so that you don't trap air under it.

Do not try to peel back the artwork from the backing paper if good contact has been made; you could easily rip or damage your work. If you must remove your artwork from backing, douse its edges with Bestine or any good rubber cement thinner. Once the artwork starts peeling away from the backing paper, squirt generous amounts of the solvent between the two sheets and the artwork should pull away smoothly. Although this method works, it's better not to have to do it at all, so take your time positioning your art correctly in the first place.

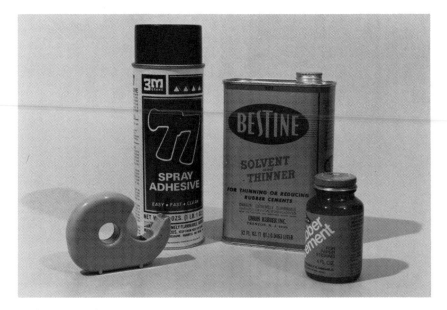

FIGURE 47. *There are several good glues available for portfolio preparation. From the left, double sticky tape, used in moderation, is good for temporary mounts. Spray adhesive is more permanent. Rubber cement thinner helps lift off improperly placed artwork or paper after it has been glued with spray, rubber cement, or tape. Rubber cement is good for temporary or permanent bonds, depending on how you apply it. Read label instructions for rubber cement and spray adhesive before applying them to your artwork.*

Once you've positioned the artwork or photo properly, cover it with tissue paper and gently burnish the surface with a rubber ruler or brayer, or with the edge of a drafting triangle. Burnishing directly onto the surface without a tissue is likely to scratch or mar the artwork.

For a less permanent bond, double-stick tape works well. When you know you'll have to remove the piece later on, use only the minimum amount of tape that will hold the artwork in place, because double-stick tape tends to get stickier with age.

Remove double stick tape from the backs of photos by squirting Bestine onto the tape. Push the tape off of the photo with the edge of a credit card or small drafting triangle.

Rubber cement is good to use on small areas or in places where spray glue can't be used. For strong, but temporary bonds, coat rubber cement on one of the two surfaces being joined, and press the pieces together. For more permanent bonds, coat both surfaces, wait until they're tacky, and join the two pieces together. Again, Bestine squirted between the rubber-cemented surfaces will ease the bond and make separating the work much easier.

The best permanent mounting technique is dry mounting or vacuum mounting. Frame shops can assist you in this permanent bonding method.

PROCESS CAMERA SERVICES

Process camera services consist of photostats, PMT's, reverses, and film positives, all of which can greatly enhance your portfolio's graphic system. The techniques, equipment, and results are entirely different from those of standard still photography, so don't confuse the two.

Process cameras have become indispensable tools for graphic designers. They are large and expensive, so they are rarely owned by individuals. But they're standard equipment in most print shops, and independent graphic designers send their process work out to these companies.

Most of the companies that specialize in process camera work are located in large metropolitan areas. They're listed in the phone book under "Photo Copying," "Graphics," or "Blueprinters." If you live in a small town, try buying photographic work from print shops or local newspapers, or from a local college or university. Many colleges offer graphic services to their students at reduced prices. Contact the audio-visual or graphic arts department.

If you find several sources for process camera work, compare prices for the same services. You may find quite a variation. Deal with the most reliable outfit that offers a reasonable price.

Photostats and PMT's — Photostats and PMT's are virtually the same. PMT is simply the Eastman Kodak Company's name for their photostat material.

Photostats are high-contrast black-and-white positives on paper. A properly done "stat' will yield a dark black image, with no grey tones, on brilliant white paper.

Photostats are primarily used to enlarge or reduce the size of an original piece of art quickly, cleanly, and cheaply. Stats are usually available in sizes as small as 8 x 10" and as large as 20 x 24". For a full page in an 8½ x 11" portfolio, you would order a standard stat size of 10 x 12". A 12 x 18" stat would be the standard size to order for an 11 x 14" binder.

Anything you want to photostat should be clean, black-and-white line artwork with no grey tones or shading. Solid black ink, rubdown lettering, felt marker lines, and black cutout paper applied to white paper all reproduce very clearly. Dark pencil lines and black ball-point pen lines reproduce fairly well, while charcoal or pencil shading and blue ball-point pen lines don't reproduce at all well.

Since photostats are so high-contrast, you can make corrections on artwork by painting over lines with type correction fluid or white tempera, or by pasting white paper over the parts of the original art you want to remove. Paste-up lines don't show up on the photostat.

With these characteristics in mind, you can soon develop an eye for what will look best as a photostat.

Technical illustrations done in ink; pen-and-ink line drawings and fashion illustrations; black-and-white logos and graphic designs; and good, dark drafting samples reproduce beautifully. Floor plans, calligraphy, cartoons, and even newspaper tear sheets photostat very well.

If you are an illustrator with lots of 18 x 24" pen-and-ink sketches and you want to convert them to an 8½ x 11" three-ring format, take your drawings to a place that makes photostats and ask for one stat of each sketch reduced to 50% its original size. They will return stats, probably 10 x 12", and your illustrations will be half their original size. You can then trim each print down to 8½ x 11". The stats will cost a few dollars each, and they should look just as sharp and clear, and probably cleaner, than your originals.

Suppose that you want some illustrations even smaller than 8½ x 11", that you want to put four drawings on a single 8½ x 11" page. Have the illustrations shot to 25% their original size, trim each stat to 4¼ x 5½", and mount them together on a single sheet of mat board.

Larger drafting samples reduce nicely to more convenient sizes, as well. When you have a drawing that's only slightly larger than your portfolio format, you can have it reduced to 90% its original size, and then the stat should fit comfortably.

Process camera measurements are given in percentages. If you want a stat shot the same size as the original, ask for a "same size" stat or a 100% stat.

Enlargements work the same way. Say that you have a small logo, an inch in diameter. If you want it two inches in diameter, ask for a 200% print. 150% will give you a logo 1½" in diameter. Be careful figuring enlargements. One artist recently wanted a small drawing reduced to postage stamp size. He was careless in figuring out the percentage he wanted and inadvertently ordered an enormous and expensive enlargement. Thereafter, he calculated his percentages with considerably more care. If you're intimidated by percentages, tell the camera person how large the original is and how large you want the image to be on the final photostat, and he will calculate the percentages for you.

Stats can also be used to get a clean, fresh-looking copy of a dogeared, smudged, or torn original drawing. The surface of photostats takes ink very well so you can modify or add to sketches, technical illustrations, or drafting samples quickly. Felt pens and ink can be applied to stats to add color, but zip films look better for large, flat areas of color or texture.

Most process cameras reduce as far as 25% and enlarge up to 200% in a single shot. But you can enlarge or reduce beyond those limits by reshooting already reduced or enlarged stats. A process cameraperson should be able to help you determine how to get what you need.

Light blue doesn't photograph on a stat, so you can write instructions directly onto the artwork without having them show on the stat by using very light blue pencil. Red will photograph as black.

If you want an image to fall in a certain place on the photostat, draw a sketch of what you want the final stat to look like and give it to the cameraperson to explain what you have in mind. For example, say that you have a logo and you want it positioned in the lower right hand corner of an 8½ x 11" page. Give them a sketch like the one below.

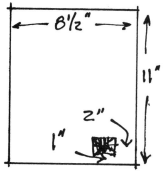

Position logo as shown
2" from right edge
1" from bottom edge
on a sheet that can
trim to 8½" x 11"

FIGURE 49

If you don't explain this clearly, you will probably get a stat with the logo centered on the paper. You will find that most stat houses are happy to give you what you need, as long as you explain your requirements. A quick sketch is the best method of explanation.

Except in unusual cases, most stat houses will have your work ready for you in one or two working days. Some places can even fill your order while you wait, but print shops or newspapers may take several days to get around to doing your stats.

Reverses — Reverses are stats in negative form. You start with an original that's black on white and end up with a white image on a black background. The effect is often more dramatic than a positive stat, but it should be used sparingly.

Reverses are especially effective when used for supplemental details in a portfolio: captions, diagrams, maps, and floor plans can all look more interesting when presented as reverses.

However, because of all the black, reverses can look too heavy and dramatic, so don't overuse them. Also keep in mind that large blocks of type in white-on-black reverse print are difficult to read. A resume, for example, would not look or read well in reverse print, whereas a one- or two-sentence photo caption would work nicely.

Reverse stats come in the same standard sizes as positive stats, and they are usually more expensive.

FIGURE 50. *The original line illustration on the right was reduced into positive and reverse prints so that they would fit in an 8½ x 11" page format.*

Film Positives — Film positives are just like positive stats, except that they're developed on a transparent film base rather than paper. Film positives are also more expensive than paper stats so restrain yourself from ordering more than you can afford.

Film positives are usually shot on polyester film rather than acetate, so you may want to punch them to fit the hole arrangement in your binder. You should also take advantage of the transparency of the film and incorporate the design of the following page into the design of the film page.

Film positives make good first sheets in a portfolio, and can protect the front page in the binder from wear and tear. Interesting photo captions that show the photo through the film and effective overlays for maps, diagrams, and designs can also be made with positives.

Since the positioning of the image is so important on film positives, it's a good idea to prepare artwork the same size as the final film positive. For example, if you want an 8½ x 11" film page with your name in type across the bottom, take a piece of illustration board or heavy art paper and draw an 8½ x 11" box on it in light blue pencil. That's your finished page. Next, rub down the type onto the exact position where you want it to fall on the film positive. Have the page shot at same size onto a 10 x 12" sheet of film. When the film positive comes back, you just trim off the excess, punch holes to match your binder rings, and put it into your portfolio.

There are many other uses for a process camera, but stats, reverses, and film positives are the ones most helpful in portfolio preparation. If you find yourself frequently using these services, check with your stat house to see what else it can do for you. Some houses are happy to give you folders with actual samples of the different services they can provide.

Variable size copiers--A much less expensive way to reproduce line art and type is to use a good quality copying machine. Models that reduce and enlarge to specific sizes are common and can add enormously to a portfolio's graphic appeal without the high cost of photostats. Most copiers will accept different kinds of paper, and many will copy in colors. An added advantage is that it is easier to get hands-on access to these machines so that you can experiment and get the results you want.

Color Photostats — Another recent development is the color photostat. It is a direct process like the black and white photostat, except that it reproduces images in full color. There are several brands on the market, each with its own set of qualities. The color and image quality is usually not as good as a photograph taken by a professional photographer, but it is usually much better than color Xerox copies; and the cost falls between the two processes. If you think that color stats would help your portfolio, investigate a source and talk to them about their capabilities, show them your work, and get their suggestions. Some of these color stats can be made from color original art, color photographs, or even color slides. Another real advantage to this service over color Xerox is the ability to change the size of the image quickly, inexpensively, and accurately.

5.
Displaying Original Artwork

As mentioned in Chapter 2, it is always more effective to display original artwork in a portfolio than to display photographs of the work. This chapter is devoted to suggestions on how you can use your original artwork in your portfolio.

ILLUSTRATIONS

As an illustrator you probably create artwork of reasonable and portable size, so you should be able to display the original pieces.

First, go through your work and select the pieces you want to show. Then go through the chosen pieces and pick out the largest, up to about 18 x 24". Anything smaller than that can be shown as original art, while

FIGURE 51. *This portfolio of work by illustrator Dugald Stermer is designed with a horizontal format, since much of the larger work is wider than it is tall. Also in this portfolio, single sheets of acetate between printed samples act as slip sheets. Unlike sheets that wrap around each portfolio page, the single sheet allows a viewer to see the actual surface of the printed page.*

anything larger will have to be reduced photographically to fit the portfolio. Larger artwork, up to 20 x 30" or so, can be shown on uniformly sized storyboards or pieces of illustration board. Illustrations larger than 20 x 30" become too difficult to carry around to interviews.

Illustrations designed to work with type to create complete graphic designs should be displayed along with the finished printed piece, which contains the type. If you're binding your work, put the printed piece on the left-hand page and the illustration opposite it on the right-hand page. This way you will draw more attention to the original, because a right-hand page has more impact than a left, as it's usually the one you see first as you turn a page.

If you're showing an illustration, but you don't like the way the finished piece came out, you can decide not to include the printed illustration; the original illustration can, of course, stay in.

Captions for Technical Illustrations — Technical illustrators frequently illustrate concepts, equipment, or processes that they themselves don't fully understand. If the drawings you're showing aren't self-explanatory, write captions for them that explain how they were used and where they were published, rather than what they were meant to explain. A caption that says, "This pen-and-ink drawing illustrates a chemical process explained in a high school biology textbook," makes much more sense to an interviewer than a technically complicated explanation of the scientific concept itself.

Drafting Projects — Large drafting samples can be shown several ways. Keep in mind that when you present a whole portfolio of drafting samples you're trying to show several distinct skills, all of which are related. You want to show that you can comprehend many elements in a project, pull them together, organize a drafting scheme, do a layout, refine it and then do a final drawing that will be blueprinted. This entire progression can be shown in a small-format portfolio by using the following method.

First, show a photograph of the part, model, or site you are working from, and follow it with a brief description of the project. Then, put together an outline, again very brief, showing the elements you had to include in the final drawing. Follow that with a very rough sketch of the final layout.

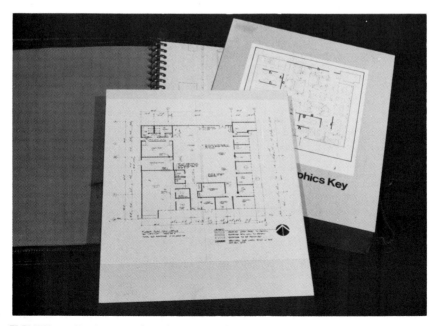

FIGURE 52. Drafting samples reduce to portfolio size as photo stats nicely.

Next, cut out a detailed section from your preliminary drawing that's the same size as your portfolio page. Then, for comparison, cut the same section from the final drawing, or from a photostat of that section. It's important to clearly show a good, detailed section of your finished drawing so that you can display your pen or pencil weight, lettering ability, and neatness.

Finally, have a loose folded blueline or printed sample of the finished drawing to present to your interviewer so that he can see the entire drawing. For the rest of your portfolio, you can show reduced Xerox copies or photostats of drafting samples rather than the actual pieces. In this way, you can display the range of your ability, without the hassle of unrolling large, cumbersome drawings during an interview. The copies should cover all of the kinds of drafting you can do, with as much variety as you think you need to show.

A portfolio as complete as the one described above is much more elaborate than most drafting portfolios, but it will also make its owner look considerably more organized and professional. A good draftsperson is much more valuable to a company than someone who's obviously disorganized or not concerned with the way they present themselves. A well-planned portfolio can emphasize your extra organizational qualities.

Freelance Architectural Illustrators — If you're about to put together a portfolio of professional architectural renderings, you already know that a client frequently gets to keep the final versions, which means you probably won't be able to show the original renderings in your portfolio.

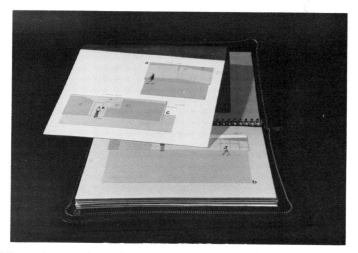

FIGURE 53. *Once you have selected a portfolio size, you can make all your presentation boards or artwork to fit the portfolio as was done here. The designer has an 11 x 14" ring binder, so she makes most of her presentation mock-ups on 11 x 14" board that can be quickly inserted into her portfolio.*

If that's the case, you'll have to render some drawings specifically for your portfolio. Make several, each done on the same size board, using a variety of techniques and media. Supplement these specially rendered drawings, which will be the substance of your portfolio, with photographs of previous work, sketches, preliminary drawings, detail sketches, and, finally, with photographs of the completed buildings. These "before" and "after" combinations can add to your reputation if the renderings you made before look just like the building after it was completed. After all, this vision is what an architectural illustrator is selling, so emphasize it.

PRINTS

Printmakers share some of the problems that art photographers face. Your finished print is your "original" artwork, so its surface is an important element in your work. You need a portfolio that will show off the surfaces of your prints.

A boxed portfolio allows you to carry the prints loose with each slipped into a folder sheet of vellum paper. This is a very simple way to protect and show off your prints. As with fine photographs, people have more respect for artwork that's slipsheeted than for work that's simply stacked and unprotected.

Be careful if you're showing prints with embossed or raised textures. You don't want to apply pressure to the surfaces of the prints, either in or out of the portfolio, since you run the risk of flattening the embossing.

Another method to protect your more valuable or delicate prints is to hinge-mount the back of each print (i.e., attach just one edge) to a sheet of mat board; then cut another sheet of mat board of the same size. Next, cut a window in the second mat board to reveal the print beneath. Cover the "sandwich" (mat board, print, mat board) with acetate. Place a caption on the back of the "sandwich," and you have a durable presentation for your print. This is the way print shows are packed to withstand handling and rough traveling.

JEWELRY

As a craftsperson who works with small, unusual, and delicate items, you have an opportunity to create special portfolios to display your wares.

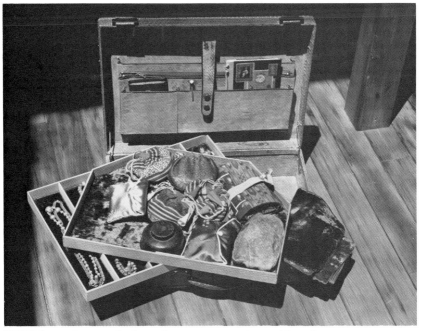

FIGURE 54. A custom-built jewelry carrying case designed by Jules Hawes serves as her portfolio of antique and ethnic jewelry. Beautifully thought out and crafted, this case holds her calculator, business cards, calendar, and address book, as well as several trays of jewelry.

FIGURE 55. Jules Hawes also makes colorful bags to protect each piece of jewelry, a touch which adds to the thoroughly professional way in which her presentations come across.

Traditionally, jewelers have displayed their goods in fine, velvet-lined boxes. This is still an excellent way to show small and precious items. If you are having a jewelry box made up specially for you, you can have it designed so that it fits into a briefcase or purse. If you're worried about the box being stolen, make it look inconspicuous, as if it weren't for jewelry.

Small bags with lots of little pockets can be easily carried, and, when made of fine leather, they become beautiful jewelry bags. Have a separate pocket for your display cloths and magnifying glass.

If you don't like to keep a large inventory but still want to show many kinds of work, supplement your bag, or jewelry box portfolio, with a standard portfolio of photographs of work you've done in the past. Photos for this kind of a portfolio should be clearly marked to show the viewer which pieces are available for sale and which ones aren't. Any photographs you take of small jewelry should be taken with a close-up or macro lens.

PHOTOGRAPHS AS ORIGINAL ART

Because of the very nature of their work, photographers can assemble examples of their skill and talent more easily than most artists: The medium in which they work is flat and small. A photography portfolio lends itself to many different graphic formats and approaches.

For example, a journalistically oriented or product photographer with prints should select a convenient size with which to work, like 8½ x 11" or 11 x 14". After he edits the photographs down to the best 15 or so, he should organize the prints into a logical order—by color vs. black-and-white, by subject matter, or chronologically. They're then ready to be bound.

If you have prints of several different sizes, select the largest and use that size to determine the size of your portfolio page. If your prints are too large for a standard size binder, have smaller prints made; since photographers usually keep negatives and transparencies from assignments, this should be easy. Most artists aren't this lucky; it would be very difficult for a painter or illustrator to remake a painting a little bit larger or smaller.

Journalistic and Product Photographs — For journalistic photographers there isn't much point showing prints larger than 11 x 14" since few magazines or newspapers can use them.

Also, journalistic photos are usually not finished products until they are printed in newspapers, magazines, or books. The surface and texture of the actual photograph is not nearly as important as the image itself. No one cares what kind of paper a Pulitzer Prize winning photograph was printed on. It's the image that won the prize. For this reason, journalistic photos can be enclosed in vinyl or acetate page protectors without detracting from them.

If you're a journalistic or product photographer, a list of publications your work has appeared in should supplement your resume. Enclose printed samples and clippings of your best published work at the end of the portfolio, after the originals. Separating them in this way helps you to play up the original photos, which are undoubtedly clearer and more attractive, while playing down the printed samples. The viewer will thus be evaluating the quality of your photos rather than the quality of a printer's work. At the same time, the clippings and printed samples at the end of the portfolio will look impressive and add to your credibility.

The same point holds true for product photographers who are showing large-format color transparencies as well as printed samples. Keep the transparencies together in the front section of your portfolio, follow that with a section of enlarged black-and-white or color prints, and finally, in a separate section at the end of the portfolio, group your clippings and publication credits.

Fine Art and Commercial Photographs — As a fine art or commercial photographer you don't have as much freedom in the ways in which you can display your work. Prints have to hold up as finished pieces of art, their surface textures being as important as the images themselves, so what kind of paper you use is important. Your portfolio must give viewers the opportunity to inspect the surface quality of your prints. Several methods can be used.

You can use a toothed binder and acetate page protectors, for as awkward as the ring arrangement may be, it does allow you to open the rings and lift off the acetate covers. Replacing the acetate onto all of the holes can create problems, though.

A nice way to show "art" photographs is to enclose them in a plain, durable box that's only slightly larger than the largest print. Slipsheet each photo with tissue paper and your photographs will usually receive more respectful handling and treatment. Without the slipsheets, though, the box of photographs looks like a jumble of old snapshots and may be treated as such.

If you choose to box your photos, pack them so they can't slide around within the box as you carry it. If your photographs don't fill the box you're using, put a layer or two of foam-core board on the top and bottom of the box to take up the extra space. (Foam-core is a rigid board made of foam sandwiched between two sheets of white paper. It's very light-weight, yet rigid enough to protect the photos. It's also a good material to use for packaging photos for mailing.)

FIGURE 56. *This photographer's portfolio is an 11 x 14" toothed binder. All of his enlargements were printed to this size. Noticé the way the two horizontal photos are falling in the same direction. An interviewer shouldn't have to twirl around your portfolio completely to see two images improperly placed in the binder.*

FIGURE 57. *Look for unusual binders. This one is a folder made for European school children. It's simple and attractively designed and makes an unusual binder for this photographer's work. He uses it to show recent prints, a cover letter, and a resume.*

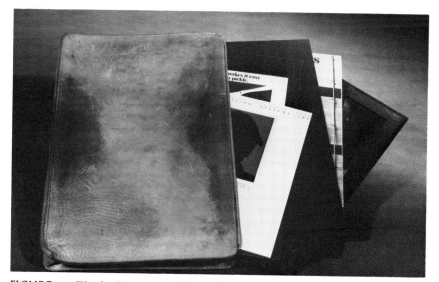

FIGURE 58. This leather case is used as a photography portfolio. Individual transparencies are mounted on matboard frames cut to a uniform 10 x 14" format. Printed photographs actually used in advertisements are flat mounted to boards, also measuring 10 x 14". Loose printed catalogs and brochures can be handed to an interviewer for closer inspection.

FIGURE 59. Individual photographs, prints, or drawings can be properly displayed and protected in frame folders made from heavy paper. The frame is covered with acetate and the photo inside is hinge-mounted like a regular print mount. A folder like this lets the interviewer see the actual surface of the print, and yet protects the photo from fingerprints, friction, and mishandling.

Slides and Transparencies — Product, commercial, and journalistic photographers who use color film for their professional work usually produce transparencies which are then converted into color separations for publication. The quality of the transparency is highest at the transparency stage, before separation and printing. Therefore, to display the photos at their best, the photographer should show original transparencies.

It is easy to display 35mm slides with slide sheets. Vinyl protectors are also available for large-format 2¼ x 2¼" or 4 x 5" transparencies, but most professional photographers prefer acetate envelopes, sandwiched between two sheets of mat board, with windows cut to the size of the image. This is a good way to display large images, especially if they are viewed on a light table with a lupe. For a good presentation, these boards can be cut to the same size and carried in a custom-fit container.

If you decide to use vinyl slide protectors for three-hole binders, use the ones that are frosted on one side and transparent on the other. Having the light diffused through the frosted plastic from the back makes looking at the slide or transparency easier, because the frosted vinyl blocks out the distracting background and softens the light.

6.
Verbal
Information

Resumes, captions, and cover letters all form the "verbal information" of your portfolio. This information should not only convey whatever it says—i.e., its contents—it should also reveal, through its appearance, your qualities as an artist.

RESUMES

Nearly everyone looking for a new job needs a resume; and for every available new job, you can safely expect at least several applicants, each with his own resume. Hence, anything you can do to make your resume more impressive and unique should enhance your chances for the job.

When a portfolio is used to help an artist find a job, it should contain both a resume bound in with the artwork and loose copies to hand out for your interviewer's files.

For most art professions, a one- or two-page resume should be sufficient to explain the important details of your education and career. Any resume over three or four pages begins to look trivial, fictionalized or both. Academic resumes are an exception to this rule since they are traditionally overstuffed with achievements.

It's usually best to put the resume toward the front of the portfolio so that an interviewer can get a general idea of your background before he sees your work.

The format of your resume should be clean, simple and well designed. There are many books on resume writing available in libraries and some have hundreds of sample resumes, each appropriate for a different situation.

Remember that a resume used in a portfolio needs to be simple enough for someone to be able to get a good idea of your experience in about two minutes, because that's about all the time an interviewer will spend looking at it during an initial interview. If you think that your career can't be fairly summarized in two pages, consider making two resumes: a brief one for your portfolio and a more complete version for the interviewer's files. Lengthy exhibition records, speaking or demon-stration engagements, awards, and publication credits would go best in such a supplementary resume.

Any resume that you hand out should be printed on a standard 8½ x 11" paper because resumes inevitably end up in file-folders. Anything much larger or smaller than that becomes difficult to file and irritating to an interviewer, and there are better ways than that to attract attention to your resume.

Using color is one way to make your resume more noticeable. Color Xeroxing is versatile and inexpensive, and a clever designer can use it to come up with colorful graphic design for his stationery. It's also possible to come up with irritatingly garish color Xerox designs, so be selective in your use of color. Experiment with the process. You may want to try several resume designs and then select the most successful rather than ordering many copies of the initial version. As neat a process as color Xerox is, the color quality is still variable enough to warrant caution.

If you're one of many applicants interviewing for the same job, you may want to include a small photograph or sketch of yourself on your resume or in your portfolio, so that the interviewer will be sure to have the right face matched to the right work. This addition is less important in less competitive situations, yet properly done it could give a more direct and personal feeling to the portfolio.

A crude line drawing might look better than a passport photo, but whatever image you select, make it appropriate to the situation. If you're applying for a teaching position, a photo showing you teaching a class would help you convey the image of yourself as a teacher more than a straight passport-type photo. A designer applying for a supervisory position should try to include a photo of himself directing other people. An illustrator could include a self-portrait illustration. A photographer needs a self-portrait photo. Give some thought to this detail and try to come up with an unusual solution to the problem of conveying the proper image of yourself.

A freelance artist doesn't really need a full resume, unless a client is really interested in hiring you as an employee. Instead, list the shows you've been in, awards you've won, your past clients, your education, publications that have featured your work, or other similar information. It's more important for you to emphasize your professional acheivements than your work experience.

PHOTO CAPTIONS

Begin thinking of how you want to caption your photos or artwork by recalling how you react to magazine photo captions. You'll probably realize that you get the most from those that are brief—a sentence or two. If your captions are clearly worded and written in a style that's consistent with the other verbal information, they will be especially helpful, and an interviewer will take the time to read them.

Captions become crucially important to the effect of your portfolio when you aren't going to personally present it.

Captions should point out important subtle information that might otherwise go unnoticed. For example, if you're writing a caption for a stained glass window, don't repeat the obvious. "This is a photograph of a stained-glass window," has wasted the reader's effort and interest. Instead, it would have been better to say: "The light is diffused by translucent glass in this seven-foot window designed for a client who wanted privacy and brilliant color in one inexpensive design." Such a caption not only sounds better but points out several less obvious design considerations as well. Always take the time to write meaningful captions.

There are a variety of ways to graphically present captions. Choose a method that's consistent with the rest of your graphics. Having film overlays with typeset words can make for a slick presentation. But typing the words yourself, using a good black ribbon on colored art paper, can be just as effective for much less money.

Use the same typewriter for all of the verbal information in your portfolio so as to avoid distracting, inconsistent typefaces.

COVER LETTERS

Cover letters introduce you and your work when you aren't able to be at an interview in person, so they should create a favorable impression with the interviewer. As with any letter of introduction, it should be brief, well written, cordial, and informative. Like a caption, it should point out the less obvious details of your work and experience.

You can use a cover letter to direct attention to an overall quality of your work or to specifics in your resume and portfolio that you would probably mention if you were at the review in person.

Cover letters are business letters and should be neatly typed. If you are sending a portfolio to someone who knows your background, a short note is all the introduction you need. You should be able to tell when a personal note is more appropriate than a formal business letter. Let the circumstances of the situation dictate your form of introduction.

CONVEYING YOUR BUSINESS
AND FINANCIAL ABILITIES

One piece of verbal information that's usually left out of a designer's portfolio is evidence of financial experience and ability in the work he does. Designers are often more restricted by their budgets than their imaginations. If the work situation you're after is one with monetary responsibilities, show somewhere in your portfolio that you can handle budgets, prices, and anticipated costs. Let your client or potential employer know that you're aware of the importance of keeping close financial control on projects. This detail becomes increasingly important as the budgets you work with grow in size and complexity. The portfolio isn't a ledger sheet, though, so limit any sample budgets to a page or so of typed information.

A budget for an interior designer might be a short list of figures showing the designer's fee; furniture costs and discounts; contract labor estimates and actual costs; and delivery expenses and totals. An architect could come up with a budget similar in detail. A graphic designer could include a co-ordination schedule for a complex printing project that might include deadlines for photographers, writers, typesetters and illustrators; printing estimates, bids, contracts, and schedules; and finally binding and delivery committments. The designer who expends the time and energy to make a schedule such as this tells anyone looking at his portfolio that he's much more than a simple board artist.

If you are looking for a job where you will be expected to perform highly technical tasks, it would be wise to show detailed technical information and your experience in dealing with complicated processes. Someone looking for a position as a ceramics instructor in an art department might include information about glaze experiments he has conducted, or unusual firing progressions, or experimental kiln designs just to quickly and effectively show that he's capable of more than throwing pots on a wheel.

If you think your portfolio could be bolstered by showing a concern for financial, business or highly technical skills, include evidence of this knowledge in your verbal information.

7.
Content Suggestions for Specific Professional Portfolios

Most basic portfolio requirements are shared by all of the art and design professions, but there are important differences. This chapter describes some of the special portfolio requirements for several different professions. Though not comprehensive, it should give you some ideas and examples that you may have overlooked.

Similar information is given in Chapter 6 for artists and designers who can use original artwork in their portfolios.

GRAPHIC DESIGN PORTFOLIOS

A typical graphic designer's portfolio includes three general categories of information.

First, a graphic representation of the artist's work experience (i.e., a resume); next, a few basic pieces that show his working knowledge of color, concept development, technical facility, and good design sense; and, finally, pieces that display the designer's special interest: illustration, advertising graphics, graphic photography, calligraphy, book design, corporate identity, cartooning, technical illustration, or whatever the designer most wants to do.

Examples of work that have appeared in print are very important to a graphic designer's portfolio. Clients or potential employers are usually more impressed with work already printed than with a piece of final artwork ready for printing, because the former shows actual experience and ability. Work that has appeared in print helps to establish a designer's credibility.

If you're a graphic designer, select pieces for your portfolio carefully and be sure to include work that shows technical facility and a working knowledge of the graphic processes involved in your field. If your work seems uninteresting because you haven't had interesting jobs, create artwork specifically for your portfolio by using some of the many graphic products available. Although they aren't printed, such samples of your talent can still display your skill.

Of all of the portfolios assembled, the graphic designer's should look the most "put together" or professional, because a portfolio is as much a graphic project as any catalog or annual report.

It should be especially well organized and graphically thought out. The craftsmanship should be refined and meticulous, and it should get

FIGURE 60. Even though an 8½ x 11" three-ring binder might be too small a page format for some artists, this graphic designer found that he could easily display several samples of his work on each page.

its point across in an interesting fashion. After all, taking disparate pieces of information and compiling them into a graphic whole is what graphic designers are trained to do. This training and skill should be apparent in the professional portfolio.

Graphic designers should also exert extra effort to produce resumes that are more graphically interesting than the standard resume. The graphic designer whose resume looks like that of an accountant isn't saying much about his talents.

Since graphic design is no less complex a field than any of the other design professions, it's likely that each designer will develop a specialty or a graphic skill that he does unusually well. Again, this specialty should be displayed in the portfolio.

As a graphic designer, don't hesitate to include in your portfolio work that you may have only had a small part in producing. Even if you only did paste-up on a large and interesting graphic project, include it with your own work, but clearly indicate exactly what part you had in the final production. Claiming credit for work you didn't do can quickly destroy your credibility and reputation as a professional.

The graphic designer looking for regular employment should also include several sketches to show a basic rendering ability; some roughs of several graphic solutions to the same design problem; and tight comprehensive layouts. Since so much graphic design is determined in the preliminary stages of a project, an employer will be looking for someone skilled in preparing roughs as well as finished mechanicals.

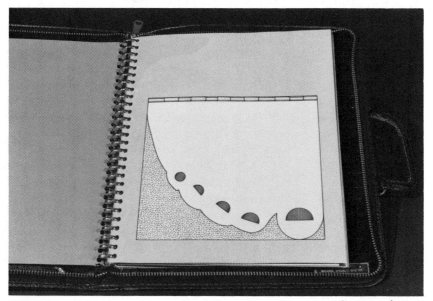

FIGURE 61. Creating original artwork and illustrations to fit your portfolio is a good way to show your abilities and skills, especially if you don't have many printed samples.

FINE ARTS PORTFOLIOS

Professional artists working in traditional media and subject matter usually find themselves within traditional marketing spheres; they are either associated with a gallery or agent or teach in an academic institution, or they hold a job and work on their art when they can. Many artists act successfully as their own agents, and a few can even convert their studios into their own galleries. But until an artist can develop a strong reputation, good gallery support, or a teaching job, he will probably find himself looking for a gallery or a good agent to represent his work, or courting agencies or individuals that give grants or commissions to fine artists. It can be a discouraging and time consuming process, but less so if you have a good portfolio to show.

As a fine artist the work itself is what you are selling; the other details of the portfolio become extraneous. If your original artwork is too large or impractical for most portfolio formats, create a portfolio around good photographs of your work.

Although it's always more expensive to have top quality photos taken of your original artwork (or to shoot them yourself and have top quality prints made), you can take some consolation in the fact that as a fine artist, who works in a consistent style, you'll need very few examples to

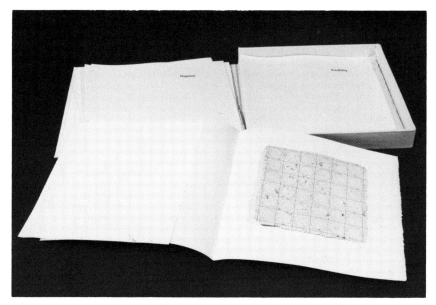

FIGURE 62. Taj Diffenbaugh Worley printed and constructed this collection of her prints and handmade paper herself. Each paper print is protected by a separate paper folder and is slipsheeted. She built the box of fabric covered cardboard and flat plates of metal. The craftsmanship displayed in this special fine art portfolio is superb.

display your talent. Your entire portfolio might consist of a few excellent color prints of recent painting; a list of awards, exhibitions, and education; any gallery announcements of shows you've had; any museum catalogs that feature your work; and lots of slides showing the whole range of your developing styles. You may not need a carefully designed graphic system, or even a complete resume.

One extra detail that fine artists should remember: occasionally an artist will assemble a portfolio of photographs and make the mistake of neglecting to include a photograph showing any kind of scale. In a photograph without a point of reference, a painting (or even a sculpture) can look tiny although it may be very large. A simple way to show the relative size of your work is to include, at the beginning of the portfolio, one print of a gallery installation of some of your typical work. Include a figure somewhere in the gallery. Such a photo will show your work in relation to physical surroundings, which will give the viewer some idea of its size. A shot of your work in your studio will also give the viewer some indication of the size of most of your work.

FASHION ILLUSTRATION PORTFOLIOS

As a fashion illustrator, flexibility, speed, and versatility are the attributes you're trying to portray in your portfolio. If you show only one style in your portfolio, you could be thought to have a very limited scope. Have a good balance of styles, types of clothes, and models in

FIGURE 63. Tear sheets or printed samples of fashion illustration can be simply presented in a three-ring binder. Keep a scrap book of all of your printed pieces, even if you choose not to include every sample in your portfolio.

your drawings. Be sure you are including men, women, children, older people, and models of different races. Vary your treatments as much as you can while maintaining a consistently high standard of drawing quality; show quick line drawings as well as tight renderings.

Use clippings and tear sheets from newspapers to show your professional experience, and put them in at the end of your portfolio, after you show the original artwork—it will give the originals more emphasis. Since fashion illustrations become dated more quickly than other kinds of illustration, don't put too much emphasis on the tear sheets, or you may look as though you aren't keeping up-to-date on the latest fashion trends.

INTERIOR DESIGN PORTFOLIOS

As an independent interior designer you'll need a portfolio as much as any other artist, since you approach new clients constantly as part of your daily business. You can use a professional portfolio not only as a tool to help you get new business, but also to make your communication with clients easier.

Going through your portfolio with a new client and noting his reactions to your past work will help you understand his likes and dislikes more clearly. You can also use the portfolio to help justify your fee, since few new clients realize how complex an interior design job can be.

A good basic portfolio for a professional interior designer might include a resume; a section on any awards and publications about your work; a section of photos of residential, commercial, and institutional spaces you've designed; and, perhaps, a few before and after shots of specific interiors. You could also include some floorplans you've drafted, some lighting and electrical diagrams, elevations, or small mock-ups showing detail work.

If you prefer industrial space planning to residential decoration, your portfolio should show that specialty clearly. If historical restoration is your main interest, the bulk of your portfolio should make this clear. Build your portfolio around your primary professional interest.

Interior design students won't have actual professional samples of work they've done and will have to rely on their student work. As a professional career develops, a student can replace his student work with professional samples.

The whole interior design profession is working to upgrade its image. Interior design is far more involved than decoration, and an interior designer can point this out with a good portfolio. If you are capable of

FIGURE 64. An attractive section divider for this portfolio was cut from an original blue-line floorplan. Rubdown type was added.

restructuring an interior space, if you can reroute plumbing, design lighting systems, handle zoning complications and municipal codes, you must display these skills in your portfolio.

PRODUCT DESIGN PORTFOLIOS

As a product designer, you have to show a variety of skills in your portfolio—at least until you develop a reputation and a good number of actually manufactured items.

If you're a young product or furniture designer, assemble a portfolio that shows many of the related skills you use in your profession. Include photos of anything you've designed that's been manufactured, as well as any prototypes of products or furniture that have not been mass-produced yet.

A couple of drafting samples, some renderings, a few tooling and manufacturing specification descriptions and accompanying budgets will help to show your general and specific knowledge of your field.

If you're looking for a position that requires several years experience, be careful how you show your drafting samples; you might be hired as a draftsman instead of as a designer unless you clearly indicate that the drafting samples are design samples.

LANDSCAPE ARCHITECT PORTFOLIOS

If you're applying for a job with a landscape architect's office or a large architectural firm, show drafting, drawing, and final rendering samples, along with photos of any gardens or grounds you've designed. Any way that you can illustrate familiarity with the horticulture of the region in which you will be working will be to your benefit.

As an experienced landscape architect looking for new freelance clients, you can usually show capability by showing photographs of many of the different kinds of projects you've worked on. A prospective client isn't as interested in your drafting ability as he is with the results of your past work.

Because of the seasonal changes of the plants and groundcovers you work with, you have an opportunity to make an interesting sequential section by showing the same garden photographed several times throughout the year, changing with the seasons in each photo. Before

FIGURE 65. Architect Jeremy Kotas put together this unusual portfolio. As an architecture graduate, Kotas collected a variety of samples of his design, rendering, renovation, model making, crafting and planning talents. He had 50 copies of each sample printed, along with cover letters, reply post cards, and folders. He mailed these packages to planning and architecture firms that he wanted to work for. The response to his efforts was gratifying. He got one of the jobs he wanted most, and nearly everyone else responded favorably to this direct and effective special portfolio.

and after photographs can also be very effective in landscape portfolios.

Unless the work you're showing is entirely structural—like pools, fountains, patios, hot tubs, out buildings, decks and balconies—use color film for your portfolio photographs. Black-and-white photos never do a garden justice.

CRAFTS PORTFOLIOS

Each craft has its own qualities. When you organize your portfolio, try to take advantage of your craft's special nature.

For example, the colors in stained glass are rich and bright. For your graphic system, you can use rich, bright colored paper. Weaving is a textural medium, so try to carry this quality into your portfolio. Perhaps your stationery or business cards can be printed on heavily textured paper; or, you could weave a carrying case for your binder. You might also include a few close-up photographs of heavily textured weavings, dramatically side-lit to emphasize this texture.

Ceramics is a highly romanticized craft. As a potter, you can take advantage of people's fascination with the process of turning dirt into art objects by somehow showing the process in your portfolio. If you work on the potter's wheel, you could have someone shoot a sequential photo series. On a single page of your portfolio, show yourself throwing a lump of clay onto a wheel, centering it, and shaping it into a lovely and graceful form. The last photograph could be of you lifting the finished pot off the wheel. In a sequence like this—using small black-and-white photographs, trimmed square and mounted on a piece of mat board—you can graphically capture the hypnotic fascination of watching a potter at work.

With any craft, the process involved captures a viewer's interest as much as the finished piece, so include in your portfolio at least a couple of photographs of yourself working. You will encourage an association in the viewer's mind between you, your craft and your objects—and that's exactly what your portfolio should do.

When you're showing your portfolio to help sell your craft objects, remember to show photos of pieces that are currently available. A shop or craft outlet wants to see what it can have to sell immediately, not what's already been sold.

If you're selling your skill and knowledge as a crafts instructor, rather than objects, then, of course, it doesn't matter if your portfolio pieces are for sale or not.

A list of exhibitions, awards, and honors, and/or a list of publication credits could be put in the front of your portfolio, where a resume would normally go. Follow that list with several sharp and very clear color enlargements of your best pieces. Caption each photo with a description of the object—its size, material, technical data, and the date when it was done. Between your original work and your photos you should cover the full range of techniques that you employ.

Seeing original artwork is always more impressive than seeing photos of the work, so if the sizes of your objects are at all manageable, put the originals into a portfolio. If your work isn't readily adaptable, try to think of an unusual way to make it adaptable. And finally, don't hesitate to make original artwork specifically for your portfolio.

PORTFOLIOS FOR TEACHERS

Though not usually required for elementary and secondary schools, a portfolio is required for most college and university teaching positions in art and design. And putting one together can be a big help even when you're looking for an elementary or high school job.

As a grade school art and design teacher, you need to show three things: that you can make good artwork; that your students can learn from you (which you show by displaying the work that former students have produced in your classes); and that you're a reliable, concerned, and a capable educator. Your portfolio can help you make these points if you've taken and kept photographs of classroom activities and projects.

Your portfolio could be a simple notebook of photographs. A photo of yourself, preferably taken with your students around you or watching a demonstration, can make an important impression. Follow that with some photos of your own work, and then with some photos of former students' work. Choose examples in many different media to prove that you can teach a wide variety of techniques.

At the end of such a portfolio, include a few lesson plans or a plan for an entire semester. With such elements, you've put together a good collection of information about your abilities that should improve your chances for employment.

College and univeristy teaching positions require more complex portfolios. Portfolios are used by hiring and review committees to select new faculty members. Since competition for these teaching positions is keen, spend enough time polishing up your portfolio.

Art and design departments can be put into two categories: a department that prides itself on hiring excellent designers and artists who are also good educators, or one that hires excellent educators who also "happen" to be good artists and designers in their own right. This is a subtle, but important distinction that you should be aware of. Find out to which category the department you're applying to belongs and structure your portfolio, resume, and interviews accordingly.

If the department is looking first for a professional designer or artist and secondly for a good educator, your portfolio should be entirely oriented to your profession. Simply mention your teaching experience in your resume and letters of recommendation.

But if the department is looking for an educator who happens to do art or design work well, the thrust of your portfolio should be on your ability to teach in the classroom and studio. Emphasize this by displaying teaching awards or honors you've been given, education workshops you've participated in or attended, and publication credits. Your own work should fairly and adequately represent your work experience, while emphasizing its educational nature.

Keep in mind that most of the larger art and design schools and departments (and many of the excellent smaller ones) usually hire professionals who can also teach for their studio classes, while hiring academics or educators for their historical or technical teaching positions. But rather than relying on pat rules, you'll have better luck getting the position you're after if you investigate the department thoroughly before you apply for the job.

If you aren't sure, when an art or design department requests a portfolio, ask them what kinds of samples they expect to see. If you're applying for a position as a weaving instructor, make sure the department isn't also looking for a beginning drawing instructor or ceramics assistant. When you know which classes you'd be expected to teach, you can tailor your portfolio to those requirements.

PORTFOLIOS FOR DESIGN FIRMS

Once you are an established professional with a design firm, your portfolio should reflect that stature. The form your portfolio takes when it represents a company rather than just an individual can be an interesting design problem.

Some designers swear by slide presentations. They say clients are more likely to be impressed with the scale and consistency of presentation when it's shown in projected slide form. The work of many designers, photographed and presented as a single body of work gives an impression of uniformity that is appropriate in professional interview situations.

Slide shows have distinct drawbacks, however. You are at the mercy of the slide projector, the light conditions of the presentation room, the length of the interview, and the quality of the slides of your work. When these variables are in check, you can have an impressive representation of your firm's abilities and acheivements. But if the conditions are poor, or if something goes wrong with the equipment, it can be disastrous.

Always try to make presentations in your own office. If you can't, check the client's office or presentation room to make sure that you can darken the room, that you have a screen or at least a blank white wall to project the slides onto, that you have electric outlets near the projector, and that you won't be interfering with a conference scheduled in the same room at the same time as your interview. It can be a risky way to make a presentation for your firm, but many designers wouldn't think of using any other method.

A printed portfolio is standard in most large architectural firms, and they are becoming more popular in interior and graphic design firms as well. Printed portfolios are usually simple folders, printed with the company name, logo, or a strong graphic design on the cover. Inside are flaps that hold individual sheets of printed pages that describe projects the firm has completed. Typically, the sheets have photos, drawings, and descriptive information about the project. When a new project has been completed, a new sheet is printed and added to the portfolio packets. These packets can be mailed or handed out to potential clients.

8.
Presenting
Your Portfolio

Armed with a splendid portfolio, you can start arranging interviews. Whether you're seeking freelance work or answering an advertisement for a job, you should plan your approach in a professional manner. First, you should find out whatever you can about the company or clients you're contacting.

WHAT TO KNOW BEFORE YOU GO

If you discover that a company is disreputable, or that an individual is difficult to work for, or that a firm has an unusually high turn-over rate, be forewarned. It's better to find out the negative aspects of the work or the personnel before you invest your time and effort in a situation that will be ultimately unsatisfactory. If you're offered a job and you have reservations about taking it, explain your reservations to the person that's hiring you and try to resolve any uncertainties before you go to work. If you don't express your doubts from the beginning, you'll find that they usually grow. By accepting the position, you've accepted the conditions that come with it. Therefore, your bargaining position is usually better before you accept the job.

Whenever you make an appointment to show your portfolio, get the first and last name of the person who will be interviewing you. Make the appointment as soon as it is convenient for both of you, and make sure you can keep the appointment. Leave a phone number where you can be reached in case the appointment has to be canceled by the interviewer. If you have to cancel, give the interviewer as much notice as possible, and try to reschedule another appointment. Never leave your interviewer or prospective client waiting for any length of time. Showing up late for an appointment is unprofessional enough; failing to show up at all is an inexcusable insult.

Time is an important element of a portfolio presentation. Plan the interview around the amount of time you can expect your interviewer to give you at your first meeting.

For example, an initial interview of a half-hour is common. Plan on spending half of that time, fifteen minutes, showing your work. Expect to spend the rest of the time discussing the position and answering his questions about your experience and qualifications.

Don't make the mistake of including so much artwork in your portfolio that the interviewer cuts you off before you're through. You can ask the interviewer whether he would like to see more samples of your work at a later time. That can be a good way of getting another interview. You can also carry a second portfolio with more samples of your work if you just aren't sure how much the interviewer wants to see.

OVERCOMING ANXIETY

Most young artists and designers, and many older ones, as well, are terrified of making presentations, being interviewed, or making an effort to push their talents. As a result, many talented artists and designers never receive the recognition they deserve. Though prevalent in any profession, this problem and attitude is especially acute in the arts.

Although art schools usually make an effort to prepare their students for the professional world, colleges and universities consider such preparation non-academic, and therefore, not proper subject matter for a liberal arts degree. This attitude is gradually changing, as it should. By failing to teach their students how to present themselves as professionals, schools perpetuate the myth that selling your talents is degrading. It's not, of course. Marketing your skills is a professional necessity, and the sooner an artist or designer can begin to enjoy the process—the sooner he can approach interviews with confidence and ease—the sooner he will be making successful presentations of himself and his work.

One art employment agency interviewer explains that she can always tell graduates of the Art Center College of Design in Los Angeles because of the way they approach an interview. The graduates arrive punctually, introduce themselves, hand her a completed application and their resume. Then they unzip their portfolio, put it in front of the interviewer opened to the first page, and walk around to the front of her desk and sit down to wait for the interviewer to ask questions about their resume or portfolio. This interviewer enjoys the neat professionalism of this kind of artist or designer because it makes an immediate good impression and speaks well of their training.

Because the interviewer sees many portfolios a week, both she and the Art Center graduates know the procedure and expect it. This approach to an interview wouldn't be appropriate for a client who rarely sees an artist's portfolio; he may not know what to do with an opened binder of artwork. This is often the case with freelance clients. If you see that you are expected to take charge and present yourself and your work—rather than having the interviewer take the lead—use your portfolio and speak as you go through it, explaining the work.

If you think of an interview as an opportunity to meet and get to know someone who will probably become your colleague in the years ahead, you'll be less intimidated by the interview. Meeting the interviewer, who usually has a similar profession to yours, isn't much different from meeting someone on a plane, at a party or a social event.

When you realize this, and when you believe that your talents are substantial, you'll begin to enjoy making presentations. They can become a rewarding part of your career.

ADVICE FROM A "PRO": DORA WILLIAMS

Dora Williams, director of Art Jobs Agency in San Francisco, estimates that she has seen literally hundreds of thousands of portfolios in the twenty-five years she's been in the arts placement business. She has several suggestions for artists and designers looking for work with their portfolios.

She dislikes looking at oversized art: artwork that doesn't fit into the portfolio case. Artists dragging large paintings or sculptures and illustrators carrying around rolls of drawings are making it hard on themselves. "Artwork in public behaves badly," she says about oversized paintings and other work people have dragged into her office over the years. She much prefers to look at slides of large work.

She wants graphic designers to show her actual printed samples. She also enjoys seeing the design and thought processes in a designer's work as shown by roughs, "comps," camera-ready art and, finally, the printed pieces. She strongly recommends including at least one full sequence showing this process in your graphic design portfolio.

Ms. Williams urges artists and designers to drop the verb "to do" and its forms from their presentation and interview vocabularies. "Artists and designers sound much more professional the moment they take this advice. Illustrators don't 'do' a book—they *illustrate* a book. Interior designers don't 'do' an office—they *design* an office. Graphic designers *lay-out* magazines, *spec* type, *paste-up* ads, and *proofread* galleys." Relying on *do, done* and *did* indicates to her that you don't consider your professional skills substantial.

She's also against the practice—common in art schools, colleges and universities—of keeping the best samples of the students' work. "Instead," she says, "schools should have the right to photograph all of the student work. Young artists and designers need every good piece of artwork they have and schools shouldn't be allowed to keep any of it."

Dora Williams uses five pieces of information to get to know the persons she interviews: their appearance, their resume, their handwriting on the application form, a half-hour interview, and a good look at their portfolio. "With those five things, I can get to know someone pretty well in half an hour."

Nine Most Commonly Asked Questions And Their Answers

Q. *How many pieces of artwork should I put in my portfolio?*
A. Usually from 10 to 20. If your work has been done in one medium, then you need about 10. If your work is in many media, then include about three samples of each style or medium up to 20. Any more than that is bound to get either repetitious or boring.

Q. *Should I leave my portfolio with an interviewer?*
A. It's not usually a good idea unless it's only for a few hours or overnight. Even then showing your own work is to your advantage. If you do leave your portfolio with a client, be sure to pick it up when the client said he'd be through with it. Never leave it longer than necessary.

Q. *How often should I update my portfolio?*
A. Constantly. Each time you do a piece, consider whether it is portfolio material. Each time you go through your portfolio, look for work to take out and ways to improve what you have.

Q. *Should I ship my portfolio?*
A. It's never a good idea to ship any portfolio with irreplaceable artwork. If you do, have it fully insured to current replacement value. Anything you value should always be sent by registered, express, or guaranteed overnight delivery, insured of course.

Q. *How do you determine the value of a portfolio?*
A. About the only way to accurately estimate the value of your portfolio is to determine how much it would cost you to recreate it from scratch. To determine that, you need to keep an accurate accounting of the materials you used: how many photo prints and slides you included, the cost of the binder, rubdown type, and photo graphics; the number of page protectors you used; and the cost of related materials like spray adhesive. Also keep track of the number of sheets of art paper and mat board that went into your portfolio.

A detailed accounting like this will help justify and verify your claim, should your portfolio get lost or destroyed in the mail.

Q. *What about the value of the artwork itself?*
A. It's difficult to collect damages on destroyed or lost pieces of artwork unless you have had the work appraised by a recognized art dealer before shipping it. As you can imagine, the process becomes complicated.

The best precaution is to pack your portfolio in an extremely well-marked, virtually indestructible shipping container or crate.

Q. *Do I have to worry about people stealing my work and ideas?*
A. Certainly, but only if you are dealing with disreputable firms or individuals. Try to investigate the reputations of the companies you will be dealing with. If you are at all suspicious, don't let your portfolio out of your sight.

Q. *Should I give my portfolio to an agent or representative?*
A. No. Instead, prepare another smaller portfolio for your agent and get suggestions on what he thinks you should include in it. A good agent or rep can be extremely helpful to you and your career.

Q. *Can I use student work in my portfolio.?*
A. Certainly. Most recent graduates have little except student work to include in their portfolio. It's a good idea to replace student work with examples of professional work as they become available.

Appendix I: Photographing Your Artwork

Unfortunately, very few artists and designers work small enough—or with materials flat, durable or lightweight enough—to make practical portfolio pieces. They have to make do with photos, drawings, and slides of their work.

The sculptor who works in bronze or cast fiberglass; the artist who paints on large canvasses; the potter; the glassblower; and the weaver all share a similar problem—they can't usually show original work because it isn't practical or convenient. Artists who work in more contemporary forms, such as conceptual, environmental, or performance art, don't even create tangible objects, which makes creating a portfolio considerably more complex. Architects, interior and fashion designers, furniture designers, industrial designers, and environmental planners all need to convert their work into a size and format compatible with their portfolio. Probably the easiest and least expensive way to do it is photographically.

Cameras—and the photo techniques you can do with them—are popular, relatively inexpensive and highly versatile tools that are becoming increasingly important for artists and designers as photography's widespread applications become more apparent and profitable.

In some of the more esoteric design circles, people believe that cameras will be as important to designers in a few years as pencil and paper are today. For some designers that's already the case. A good many design departments in colleges and universities have added photography to their list of required design courses, not so much to turn design students into professional photographers, but rather to familiarize them with photography as an important visual communication tool.

One of the most helpful designer uses of the camera is in portfolio preparation; but no matter what the use, the artist or designer who is familiar with cameras and photo techniques is bound to be able to communicate visual ideas better than one who is not.

DOCUMENTING CHANGE AND PRESERVING WORK

Each artist works differently, of course, but some artists discover that the more involved they become in their profession, the more quickly their work grows and changes. By getting into the habit of consistently photographing your artwork, it's possible to illustrate your artistic growth—something that isolated pieces of artwork alone can't show.

By successfully documenting and compiling examples of something as abstract as growth, you're putting your portfolio in a class apart from everyone else's. You've emphasized a creative direction, which is an important point in your favor that certainly should be shown in your portfolio.

Though any photograph of a piece of artwork is better than none at all, good photographs are considerably more helpful. Chances of the photograph being a good one are better if the photo is taken when the piece is in its best condition—usually when the piece is new. Delicate objects are frequently victims of careless handling or improper storage, and even sturdier sculptural pieces might never look as good as they do right after they are finished. Wood can crack; paint can discolor or peel; dings and chips from rough treatment can occur. Some metallic work, aging gracefully and covered with its patina, does look better with age, but most work—especially contemporary work—looks better when its fresh.

Another reason to photograph your artwork as soon as it's completed is that it may be your only chance. If the work is sold, you may never even see it again. If the work is a drawing, print, painting, or a fine illustration, it may be framed and put under glass—which makes photographing the work all the more difficult.

Designers are wise to do the same. Interior designers should photograph interiors immediately after finishing them, since they're often quickly changed by the client. One interior designer returned to a restaurant that he had designed in a distinctly 1900's style to discover (to his horror) that a large portion of the restaurant had been converted into a contemporary discoteque. Fortunately, he had taken enough photographs of his original plan so that he could still include the unaltered restaurant in his portfolio. Many other designers are less fortunate.

Another designer had similar trouble with an office she designed. New management moved in and changed her design beyond recognition. She had only two murky snapshots to show for her efforts, neither of which did justice to the work.

Fashion and costume designers work with materials that are usually very susceptible to damage. If you make one-of-a-kind pieces, you have the same problem as artists who sell their work: it's entirely possible you'll never see your work again, and never have an opportunity to photograph it.

Photography for most architects requires additional thought. You'll want photographs of your work in various stages of completion, with the final results well documented. Landscape architects and environmental designers often need photos taken over a long period to show how their work grows with age and changes with the seasons.

SLIDE PORTFOLIOS

Some art juries and most graduate schools review the work of their applicants by requesting slide portfolios. Sometimes they are very specific in their format requirements, asking that you send no more than, say, twelve slides of your work. This process of evaluation by slides has advantages and disadvantages.

Obviously a slide portfolio is inexpensive; mailing slides costs considerably less than shipping works of art. Also, slides are more convenient for both artists and jury or committee members, especially when the work of many artists must be reviewed. If you're applying at several schools or competitions, you can mail duplicates of your slides to several places at the same time, which can be a real advantage.

Slides can be great equalizers as well. Since each slide submitted will be viewed by each judge under the same circumstances, no one artist

FIGURE 66. Vinyl slide pages make filing and locating transparencies easier for files and slide portfolios.

should start off with any great advantage. In theory, each artist is judged by the merits of the artwork alone—as represented by the slides.

Unfortunately, not every piece of artwork can be photographed with equal success. A quiet and beautifully subtle lithograph is likely to lose some of its flavor when photographed, while a massive bronze piece will reproduce fairly well in a slide. Visually bold and strong pieces tend to photograph better, and this is probably the chief disadvantage of judging artwork by slides.

As popular as the slide method of jurying is now, it will probably become standard practice in the years ahead. If you're applying for graduate school, entering a contest, or submitting your slides for whatever reason, the following steps can help you improve your chances:

1. Send only your very best slides.

2. Send slides that *accurately* represent your work. Juries frequently do their initial selection by slides and their final jurying from the original work, and judges do not hesitate to reject work that was inaccurately represented by its slide.

3. Clearly mark your slides, giving complete information, such as your name and the top front of the slide. Also, include a supplemental written list containing this information so that a judge can read the information while he's looking at the projected images. Always include the dimensions of the work, as well as the medium. (See Chapter 8.)

4. Clean and dust your slides before sending them.

5. If the photo lab you use returns your slides in cardboard mounts, you may want to remount your best slides in plastic ones. Cardboard gives the edge of your projected slide a fuzzy, shaggy appearance, while plastic mounts project sharp and clean edges. Though not a crucial point, it's a professional touch. Avoid sending slides in glass mounts, because some projectors cannot show them.

6. Mask out distracting background details, using metallic mylar tape especially made for the purpose.

7. Package your slides securely to protect them from shipping damage. Placing your slides in a plastic slide protector page, sandwiched between two sheets of cardboard, is a safe way to mail them.

8. Include a stamped, self-addressed return envelope with your slides to insure that they will be returned to you promptly after jurying.

9. Send good-quality duplicates whenever possible; if you must send the originals, keep duplicates for yourself. Never send your only copy of an important slide—don't assume that the person looking at it will be as careful handling it as you are.

10. Try to shoot a three-dimensional object from an angle that best describes the piece, but send more than one view of the piece if that's what it takes to represent it fairly. This is as important for architectural models as it is for sculpture.

11. Before you mail them, always project your slides or carefully inspect them with a lupe to check them for clarity, focus and general impact. Flaws are much more noticeable in slides when they're projected than when they're only held up to a light.

12. When one slide of an entire piece doesn't do the work justice, send close-up detail slides. Clearly mark them as detail slides so that they are not judged as separate entries.

13. Keep a record of when and where you send your slides so that you can locate them if they aren't promptly returned. Slides are small

enough to be easily misplaced and unintentionally forgotten, so you may need to send a reminder to get them back.

GETTING READY TO PHOTOGRAPH

If you produce flat artwork like paintings, prints, drawings, floorplans, sample boards, or graphics, and if you know you're going to have to photograph them regularly to get slides or enlargements for your portfolio, you might decide to set aside a corner of your studio as a photo area. If several artists who could use this area pooled some money, it becomes an inexpensive and invaluable proposition. Although crafts and small three-dimensional work require a little more equipment, divided among several craftspersons, artists, architects, or interior planners, the expense is still minimal. College art and design departments could do their students a great service by installing small photo areas where students could document their work.

With even the most basic set-up, using very inexpensive equipment, it's not difficult for you to produce professional-looking slides that accurately represent the artwork.

Basic Photo Equipment

The basic photo equipment you'll need includes: a camera; film; a tripod and cable release; a light meter; an 18% grey card; lights, reflectors, and lightstands; and backdrop paper, tape, tacks and props.

Camera — An increasing number of design departments in colleges and universities require that their students learn to take good photographs with 35mm cameras. Most insist on 35mm cameras for several reasons—they're extremely versatile; film, lenses, filters and accessories are widely available; the quality of the photography can be very good; and although the camera itself can be expensive, film and processing is reasonable.

Larger format cameras, like 2¼ x 2¼", 4 x 5" and 8 x 10", are for the professional photographer, as the cost of film and processing alone puts them out of the price range of most amateur photographers.

Smaller cameras and "Instamatics" are designed to take snapshots rather than high quality photographs. As convenient as "Polaroids" may be, the results are limited to a single-size print of marginal to dismal quality. Polaroid makes some fine products for professional photographers, but for most of the work artists and designers do, a good 35mm camera is a much better investment than a snapshot camera.

You need an adjustable camera so that you can control shutter speed, focus, lens opening, and light setting.

If you have a 35mm camera, it's one of two kinds: a rangefinder or a single-lens reflex (abbreviated SLR). With a single-lens reflex model, when you look through the viewfinder, you're looking through the actual lens of the camera. Whatever you frame in your viewfinder will be on the film when you trip the shutter. An SLR is an easier camera to use because each time you change lenses or add filters, your eye sees what the film will capture.

With rangefinder cameras, on the other hand, when you look at your subject, you look through a window that shows you approximately what the film will record. If you change lenses or add filters, you have to imagine how that is going to effect the shot. Still, if you have a rangefinder camera, you should be able to take fine photographs of your artwork.

If you're about to buy a camera, you'll probably find single-lens reflex models much easier to learn to use. If you're going to use your camera to photograph very small objects like jewelry, you should certainly use a single-lens reflex camera, because with small details or objects, you must be able to see exactly what will appear on the film.

If you're a jeweler, or if you do very small work, you will need a set of close-up lenses or a macro-lens. You add close-up lenses to your regular lens whenever you want to take a picture a few inches from the subject. A macro-lens takes extreme close-up shots and regular, normal-distance shots up to infinity. Macro-lenses have become important tools for some artists and designers.

Film — There are a number of films on the market, and it's important for you to know what to expect from each so that you can select the film most appropriate for your needs.

There are two basic kinds, of course: black-and-white and color.

Most black-and-white films are negative acting, which means that you get a transparent negative image when the film is developed. It is from these negatives that prints or enlargements are made. Prints can be as small as the individual frame on the film itself, or as large as a wall mural. For portfolios, prints usually range from 5 x 7" to 11 x 14", and can go up to 14 x 22".

Each black-and-white film has important characteristics. Some films are fast, meaning that it doesn't take much light to fully expose them. They're handy in low-light situations without a flash. These films tend to be grainy, and enlarged prints from grainy film show a sandy texture on the surface of the subject. Some photographers work for grainy effects, while others find that they distract from the real image. Kodak's Tri-X is a fast film; it has an ASA rating of 400.

Other films are very slow, meaning that it takes lots of light to fully expose them. They're most often used outdoors on bright days. Their chief advantage is that they're fine-grain films that can be blown up enormously without producing a distractingly grainy texture. Kodak's Panatomic-X falls into this category; it's rated as ASA 32, so it's a very slow film.

In the middle range, with pretty fine grain at a faster speed than the slow films is Plus-X. It's ASA is 125, so it's fast enough for most normal indoor and outdoor lighting situations. This versatile film is a good one for most amateurs to use to photograph their artwork.

Color Films — Working with color film can be more complicated only because color is such a variable element. Since color is determined by the light in which it is seen, and since types and sources of light vary dramatically, a single type of film will not satisfactorily reproduce every kind of color in every kind of light. For accurate color reproduction, you need to match the film to the light source.

Daylight film is used when the primary source of light is the sun or a flash or strobe light. *Tungsten film* is used when the primary light falling on the subject is tungsten or incandescent light.

While the two kinds of light may not change the colors of things much to our eyes, they can change them markedly on film.

Fluorescent light is very difficult to use in color photography, so it's best to avoid trying to accurately reproduce color with it.

Color photos taken with unfiltered fluorescent light often come out looking extremely blue-green, as do shots taken with tungsten film in daylight. The opposite happens with daylight film used with tungsten light: the colors are much too warm in tone. Whites are replaced with deep yellow, and blues nearly disappear. The only way to photographically reproduce the colors in your painting correctly is to match the film to the type of light you're using and to avoid photographing under fluorescent light whenever possible. Filters that convert fluorescent light to daylight or Tungsten-light temperatures are available, but the results are still usually less than satisfactory, primarily because there are too many kinds of fluorescent bulbs used in fixtures to allow for easy matching of filters to bulbs.

Both daylight and Tungsten films are available in slide and negative forms. The slide film is a direct positive film: what you put into your camera is what comes back to you from the photo lab as slides. Print film is a negative film: prints are made from the negative film you put into the camera.

You can tell which kind of film you are buying by the endings in the brand names. Any color film ending with the suffix "chrome" indicates that it's a slide film. Any film ending with the suffix "color" is a negative film. It follows, then, that Ektachrome, Kodachrome, and Fugichrome are all slide, or transparency films. Kodacolor and Vericolor are negative, or print films.

FILM	FILM SPEED	PRODUCT	LIGHT USED	CHARACTERISTICS
TRI-X	ASA 400	Black & White negatives for prints	Any light	Good for low light situations. Grainy enlargements. A good fast film.
PLUS-X	ASA 125	Black & White negatives for prints	Any light	Good general purpose film. Fine grain at moderate speed.
PANATOMIC X	ASA 32	Black & White negatives for prints	Any light	Very fine grain. Slow.
EKTACHROME 50	ASA 50	Color transparencies	Tungsten. Incandenscent with **correction filter.**	Excellent indoor slide film, using proper lights. Fine grain.
EKTACHROME 100	ASA 100	Color transparencies	Daylight, strobe, or flash	Excellent outdoor slide film. Fine grain.
EKTACHROME 160	ASA 160	Color transparencies	Tungsten. Incandescent with correction filter.	Faster than Ektachrome 50. Good for hand-held indoor shots, interiors, or gallery situations.
EKTACHROME 200	ASA 200	Color transparencies	Daylight, strobe, or flash	Good for low light daylight shots or fast action shots.
Vericolor III Professional "S"	ASA 100	Color negatives for prints.	Daylight, strobe, or flash	Good for color prints shot in daylight. Good general color print film.
Vericolor II Professional "L"	Variable ASA	Color negatives for prints.	Tungsten light or daylight	Good for color prints of artwork shot in tungsten light.

FIGURE 67

Tripod — Even an inexpensive tripod is better than no tripod at all. Because the photography of artwork requires long exposure times, you'll need a tripod to hold your camera steady. Inexpensive tripods are usually very lightweight and unsteady; they jiggle during an exposure. Tying and suspending a gallon plastic bottle of water from the neck of the tripod will make it steady. Tripods are required for all exposures taken at more than 1/30th of a second.

A Cable Release — This helps prevent jiggling the camera while you press the shutter. It's necessary for any tripod shot.

A Light Meter — Many cameras have built-in light meters. If you already have a reflective light meter it will work well for artwork as long as you use it in conjunction with a grey card. If your camera doesn't have a light meter you'll need one. Hand-held meters come in two types: incident and reflective. The incident meter has a ping-pong-ball-like

FIGURE 68. *Two common types of light meters are incident, on the left, and reflective, on the right. The meter on the left measures the light falling on the subject. The reflective meter measures the light reflecting off of the subject. If your camera has a built-in lightmeter, it is reflective.*

sphere attached to it; the reflective meter doesn't. Incident light meters are usually more expensive. Either meter can be used to photograph artwork, although incident light meters are probably easier to use.

18% Grey Cards — If you use a reflective light meter, like the kind built into most cameras, you'll need an 18% grey card to help you get more accurate color in your color slides. They cost a couple of dollars and are available in larger camera stores.

Lights and Reflectors — As mentioned earlier, the lights you use must be matched to the color film you use. You have to buy lights that are rated at the same color temperature as the film you are using.

For example, if you use Ektachrome 50, a good film for the photography of artwork, you'll be using a film balanced for 3200° Kelvin light, which means that your lightbulbs should be rated to 3200° Kelvin. (With tungsten films, a 3200° K. light sources must be used to achieve accurate color rendition. Other photo lights, such as strobe lights and flash bulbs are balanced for daylight films. The advantages of 3200° K. bulbs are relatively low cost and the fact that you can see the light—and thus have more control—because they remain on, while strobes or flashes are on for an instant only.) Camera stores usually stock, or can order, inexpensive screw-in type lightbulbs that have a color temperature of 3200° K. They don't last for more than a few

FIGURE 69. An 18% neutral grey card is used to give you accurate light readings for color slides using built-in or hand-held reflective light meters.

FIGURE 70. Inexpensive clamp light reflectors make good general purpose photo lights. For color slides, buy 3200°K lightbulbs from photo stores.

hours, so don't use them as regular lightbulbs, and keep replacements handy.

Aluminum bowl reflectors with grip clamps on the back are available in hardware stores for a few dollars each. The grip clamps allow you to use chairs, tables, and bookcases as convenient light stands.

Light Stands — For frequent use, crudely fashioned lightstands made from 1 x 2" strips of wood about six feet tall and attached to a sturdy base will do very well.

Backdrop Paper — Seamless photo paper, sold in ten-foot-wide rolls, is the standard professional backdrop material. It may be too expensive for infrequent use, and it's not necessary at all for very small objects. If a white or brown backdrop is adequate, butcher paper or brown wrapping paper in a six-to-ten-foot length will provide you with a very inexpensive backdrop.

Many amateur photographers make the mistake of getting too "arty" or textural with their backgrounds. Backdrops should be entirely subordinate to the artwork itself, so choose your backdrops carefully. Velvet, burlap or satin can look gaudy and unnecessarily dramatic. Sticking to neutral or subdued colors will enhance the artwork.

Objects or artwork with fine detail or subtle tonal changes often benefit from very dark backdrops. Architectural mock-ups convey more realism when they are photographed against backgrounds that approximate those of the actual site: sky blue, grass green, concrete or asphalt grey, and so on.

Miscellaneous Supplies — Masking tape, pushpins, clamps, staples, or whatever you need to hold your work in place while you shoot it, are necessary supplies. You'll also need some white cardboard or aluminum foil taped to cardboard to help reflect light into any distractingly harsh shadows you get on three-dimensional objects you will be shooting. A table about waist high or shorter to act as a stand for your smaller art objects is also needed.

If you are shooting with color films, you'll have to block out the sunlight in your photo area, since you'll use only Tungsten light. If it's not practical to block the light from the windows, you will have to shoot your slides at night, when the outside light is no longer a problem. You'll also need to turn off all flourescent lights while you're shooting.

With black-and-white film, you can use any combination of light sources without affecting the results.

PHOTOGRAPHING FLAT OBJECTS

Unless your work is very small, it's usually easier to photograph flat artwork on a wall rather than on the floor. Most tripods aren't adjustable or flexible enough to be positioned so that the legs aren't in the picture frame. You want a wall that has as much unobstructed space in front of it as possible. If you're photographing a stretched painting, you'll want to use a wall on which hanging hardware can be installed.

Preparing the Artwork — The artwork should be removed from any frame, glass, or mat.

Hang, tack, or tape the artwork, low enough on the wall so that the center of the artwork is as high as the lens of the camera on the tripod. The next step in the procedure requires moving lights and extension cords, so move your camera and tripod to a safe location until you need to position it.

Positioning the Lights — If your artwork is small and flat and without texture, you want evenly distributed illumination over its entire surface, so as to eliminate hot spots, dark areas, and harsh shadows. Remember that the farther the lights are from the artwork, the more even the illumination will be. You also want to keep the angles of both lights consistent with one another. The height of the lights and their distance from the artwork must be equal, as well.

To determine the proper position for your lights, find the vertical centerline of your artwork, bring that line down to the floor, and continue it along the floor (your camera will be centered along that line.)

Next, bisect at 45 degrees the two 90-degree angles that are formed at the intersection of the floor-line and the bottom of the wall, and bring those lines out from the wall. You'll position your lights along these lines at equal distances from the artwork, so that a line from one light to the other is parallel to the wall.

Your lights must now be centered to the center of your artwork. If the horizontal center of your artwork is 48″ from the floor, place your lights 48″ above the floor. (The center of your lens should also be 48″ from the floor.)

With your lights in proper position, you now have to aim them so that they are bathing the surface of the artwork with light. If you were to aim both lights at the center of the artwork, you would have a photograph with a bright center and dark edges, which isn't what you want. Instead, aim the light on the right side of the picture to a point approximately one-third of the way in from the left edge of the artwork; aim the left light at a point one-third of the way in from the right edge. If your lights are far enough away from the artwork (and you have carefully placed them as described), your artwork should be evenly illuminated.

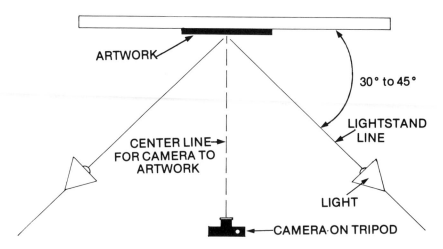

FIGURE 71. *Shooting flat artwork moves more quickly if you mark your photo area with centerlines and lightstand lines. Drawing or taping them directly onto the floor and wall is the easiest way, but taping string in position will work for temporary lines.*

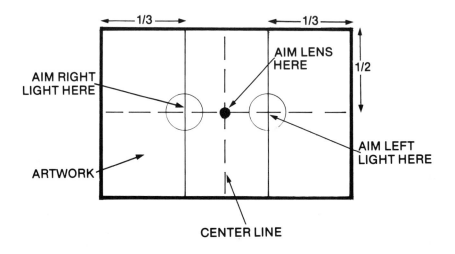

FIGURE 72. *Aim your lights to the horizontal center line of the artwork, and to opposite points one-third of the way in from each vertical edge as shown. This cross lighting will help bathe the surface of the artwork with even illumination.*

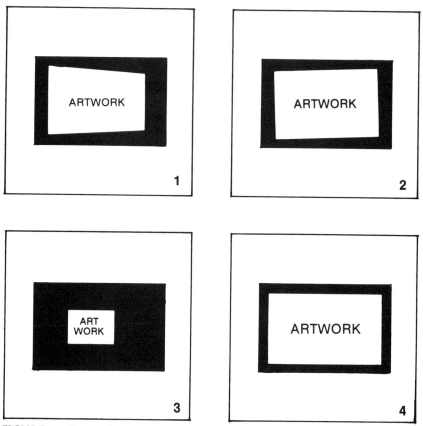

FIGURE 73. Position the image carefully; if it is crooked in the viewfinder, it will be crooked on the slide as well. Common positioning problems include:

1. Trapazoidal image. Film isn't parallel to artwork. Move Camera to correct.
2. Tilted image. Camera isn't level to edges of artwork. Adjust camera on tripod or tilt artwork to correct.
3. Image too small. Move camera closer to artwork.
4. Properly framed image. Camera is correctly positioned.

Checking the Lighting — To test for even lighting , tack or tape a sheet of plain white, brown, or grey paper over the entire artwork. Take your light meter or camera (if you're using the lightmeter built into your camera) and hold it about 6" from the paper cover. Move the light-meter slowly across the entire surface of the artwork, carefully watching to see if the needle on the light-meter changes position. If it does, then one section of the artwork is receiving more light than the other, and it will appear as a hotspot on the finished photo. Reposition the lights and make the test again.

Test the light carefully, because it's difficult for the human eye to accurately distinguish between even and uneven illumination in the studio, although the difference will be obvious on the finished photograph.

If you're using an incident (or ping-pong-ball-type) meter, you won't need to cover the artwork with paper. Instead, point the white sphere toward the camera lens and move the meter back and forth across the artwork, again watching to see if the needle moves.

Once you've determined that artwork is evenly illuminated, remove the paper cover and take your light reading from the 18% grey card.

Determining the Exposure — If you're going to use your camera's light meter to determine the exposure, you should take a light reading before you position your camera.

Set the f-stop on your camera to its smallest setting: f16 or f22. Then, take your camera and 18% grey card up to the artwork and, holding the card (grey side to the light) parallel to and a few inches in front of the work, take a light reading with the camera about six inches from the grey card.

Adjust the shutter speed rather than the f-stop to the proper exposure. Remember this reading, because as long as your lights remain in the same position, you will use it to shoot all the artwork you have ready. If you move the lights, you'll need to take another reading and adjust the camera accordingly.

If you're using a hand-held, reflective light meter, take the 18% grey card and the light meter up to the artwork. Hold the grey card in front of the artwork and point the light meter at the grey card to take the light reading—you want to know how much light is reflecting off of the grey card. Using the smallest f-stop your camera has, set your shutter speed to what the light meter indicates will give you the proper exposure.

The reason you are taking a reading with an 18% grey card, rather than from the artwork itself, is you want to know how much light is hitting the artwork rather than how much light is reflecting off it.

Incident light meters measure this automatically, since they measure light *hitting* the subject rather than the light *bouncing off* the subject, so 18% grey cards are unnecessary. With an incident light meter, point the white plastic sphere toward the lens, take the reading, and adjust the camera accordingly.

You'll want to shoot using long exposure times and a small f-stops to give you maximum depth of field and the sharpest possible edges on the artwork.

The next step is to set the camera in front of the artwork—squared, centered, and positioned so that the artwork is properly framed in the viewfinder. Take the time to do this step properly, because unless you square the camera to the artwork you will get a trapizoidal image instead of a rectangular one.

To center the image, you must position the lens to the center of the artwork. The most accurate way to do this is to position the camera directly over the 90-degree line you established when you positioned the lights. Move it along that line until the image is comfortably positioned in the viewfinder. If the image is tilted, adjust the tripod or the camera or both, until the artwork is square in the viewfinder.

Finally, tighten any adjusting screws on your tripod to keep the camera in place; be careful not to move the camera in the process.

Shooting the Photos — When you're satisfied with the way the image is positioned in the viewfinder, recheck your exposure and make sure the camera is correctly focused. Shoot the photo by carefully squeezing the cable release without jiggling the camera.

If you're shooting slides, expose at least as many frames as you will need slides. If you're making negatives, either color or black-and-white, it's always a good idea to bracket your exposures. Bracketing means you shoot one frame that's a little overexposed, according to your light meter; one frame just as your light meter tells you; and one that's slightly underexposed. By shooting like this, you can be certain that at least one of the three shots will be accurate, even if your light meter isn't absolutely accurate, or your camera shutter is a little slower than it's supposed to be.

Bracket by moving the f-stop ring one setting past or one setting before the proper setting—or change your shutter speed by one setting each way.

For example, let's say you want three perfect slides of a drawing and your light meter indicates that the proper exposure is f22 for ¼ second. You would first shoot three exposures at f22 for ¼ of a second. Then you would move the shutter speed to 1/8 second, keeping the f-stop at f22. Finally, you would change the shutter speed to ½ second at f22 and shoot three more exposures. The results should be nine slides, three properly exposed, three underexposed, and three slightly overexposed.

Bracketing is the easiest way to make sure you have compensated for minor inaccuracies in your photo equipment, or the film you're using. It's a standard practice among professional photographers. Amateur photographers object to bracketing because it seems like such a waste of film; but shooting six shots more than you need to get three good ones is not very expensive, and if you really want excellent photographs of your artwork.

Preparing for the Next Shot — You can save yourself a lot of preparation time on subsequent shots if you have artwork that's the same size as the first, so that it can be placed in exactly the same position. Until the artwork changes size (or until you have to reposition the lights) all of your initial adjustments should remain the same.

Shooting Flat, Textured Objects — If you have an embossed print, weaving, bas-relief, or other piece of textural artwork, you probably want the texture emphasized rather than flattened in the photos. To bring out the texture, move one or both of the lights closer to the wall so that the light *rakes* the surface of the artwork and creates more distinct shadows.

Check the results of your lighting arrangement carefully in the viewfinder. Slight changes in the position of the lights can dramatically alter the way the texture of the piece appears. You may discover that by raising one of the lights, the texture is more pronounced. Perhaps by moving one light back a little, a section of the texture is less noticeable. With textured but flat artwork you have to play with the lights as though you were shooting a three-dimensional object. Watch carefully how the light works with your piece, and you'll learn what kind of lighting set-ups are best for your objects.

Difficult Flat Pieces — In some ways it's harder to get a good photo of a flat object than a sculptural one. Dark pencil lines, heavily varnished paintings, flat display boards with many photos and different kinds of textures all reflect light in a way that's difficult to shoot. You'll have to move the lights around until the reflections are softer, smaller, or not noticeable. For some work, polarizing camera filters help cut down some of the reflections, and for extreme reflection problems, polarizing filters for your lights are available. If you want to get a good shot of reflective artwork without spending money on expensive equipment, all you can do is play with the positions of the lights.

Flat pieces that are too large to properly illuminate in the studio can be photographed successfully outside using daylight or any black-and-white film. Slightly overcast days will give you more even illumination. Photograph around noon-time and the color rendition of your color photos and slides will be more accurate. Keep in mind, though, that it's difficult at any time to get accurate color rendition outdoors.

PHOTOGRAPHING THREE-DIMENSIONAL OBJECTS

Photographing three-dimensional art objects is a profession all its own, full of subtleties, technique, and years of training. A good book on the subject is listed in the bibliography. Using this book as a guide, you can learn techniques that will help you take photographs which are works of art in their own right.

If all you want to do is take good, accurate slides and photographs of three-dimensional work without spending lots of money on special equipment, don't be discouraged—it isn't difficult to learn to take good photos using inexpensive equipment in a primatively arranged studio. And, because few artists and designers even try to take good photographs of their work, any extra effort you put into your photos should pay off.

About the only differences between photographing three-dimensional objects and flat objects are the composition of the image within the frame and, of course, the lighting of the object.

Lighting — Light determines how the eye perceives an object, so you can alter the form of an object by altering the way the light hits it. With art objects, you want accurate representations of the work, and therefore you will want a lighting set up that will emphasize the shape of the object with out exaggerating or distorting it.

To properly photograph a three-dimensional object, you'll need at least three different lights. The "key" light is your main light. A "fill" light is usually placed so that it fills the harsh shadows created by the key light. The "shadow," or background light, illuminates the background the object is resting upon and thereby determines how the rest of the composition is going to work. All three lights are important, so watch how each affects the entire picture.

Aluminum foil reflectors make excellent, inexpensive fill lights by reflecting light from one of your main lights to the area of the piece you want to highlight.

If you're shooting black-and-white film, you can use any combination of lights available—daylight, flourescent, small desk lamps, and even flashlights. Clamp-type reflectors are handy because they can be clamped to bookcases, chairbacks or anything else that will work as a light stand. The more manueverable your lights are, the better control you have on the lighting of the art object.

Color shots will require 3200° K. lights and Tungsten film if you want accurate color.

For a natural-lighting effect, you'll have to place the lights above eye level, since most natural lighting comes from above. Fill and highlight lights can shine from below so as to bring out details in shadowed areas.

Most art objects look best when photographed on a sheet of seamless backdrop paper that is tacked to a wall and draped in a gentle curve over the photography table. Properly positioned and framed in the camera, the object will look as though it were in a color field, uninterrupted by horizon lines and seams.

For color work, subdued-color backgrounds are more flattering to most pieces than brilliant or garish backgrounds. As a rule, select colors for backgrounds as you would choose color for mats for flat artwork, and avoid heavily textured backgrounds.

Rules of contrast apply here too. A very dark object will separate itself from a lighter background just as a white object shows up more distinctly when photographed on darker backgrounds. As an amateur, you should stick to the basic rules of contrast for reliable results.

Place the object on the seamless paper and then decide from which angle the piece should be lighted and photographed. Move the lights around, changing their heights and distances until you've found the most satisfactory lighting set up. Keep in mind that you're trying to get an accurate photograph of the artwork. Avoid overly dramatic or theatrical lighting.

Once you have the artwork and background properly lighted, and the shadows working with the piece, place the camera close to the artwork to get your light reading. Put the grey card in front of the object and bring your camera within a foot of the object and card to take the exposure reading. If you're using a hand-held reflective light meter, hold it a foot from the grey card. Incident meters should be held in front of the object, with the white sphere pointed toward the camera lens. Be careful not to shadow the light meter or grey card when determining the exposure.

Since you will want to position your camera close to the object to make your shot, and since you will also want as much of the piece in focus as possible, you should use f16 or f22 and adjust your shutter speed accordingly so that you get the greatest possible depth of field.

Framing the object in the camera is the last step before taking the picture. Position your camera and tripod far enough away from the object so that it doesn't look crowded in the viewfinder, yet close enough so that you can see the details of the artwork. Logically, if you're shooting a vertical object, you should shoot the photograph vertically and vice versa with horizontal pieces.

Compose the photograph carefully. When looking through the viewfinder, take an extra moment to think about how you're lighting and framing each shot. Visualize how the finished photo will look. Film and processing isn't so expensive for 35mm film that you can't afford to experiment. Take many more shots with different lighting set ups than you actually need, and you're more likely to end up with at least one excellent shot of your artwork.

Again, remember that photography of artwork is its own art form. If you are interested in the field, check out some of the books mentioned in the bibliography for good introductions to an interesting specialization.

Appendix II: Processing, Editing, and Displaying Photos and Slides

It's common practice for an amateur photographer to drop off a roll of black-and-white film at a camera store and to get back 20 or 36 black-and-white 3 x 5 prints. Unless the photos were snapshots, and therefore you didn't expect good quality, it's common for the results to be disappointing. When black-and-white film is sent to a large lab, a machine usually develops your prints, and the results are generally uniform, but of mediocre quality and not very flattering to your subject.

Working with Contact Sheets

Another method of working with black-and-white and color films is to request that the lab develop the film and provide you with a contact sheet. You should get back your negatives and a larger sheet of photo paper that contains strips of small prints of your negatives. From this contact sheet you can select the most successful shots and then decide which ones you want enlarged to 5 x 7" or 8 x 10" prints.

First, mark up the contact sheet to indicate the images you want enlarged by writing the numbers of the negatives chosen and specific instructions on the back of the contact sheet. Then return it to the photo lab with the negatives. Prints chosen this way will have better quality, and since you can include cropping instructions, they'll have better composition as well.

Editing and Correcting Your Slides

When your slides have been returned by the photo lab, go through them carefully. Put them into a projector or viewer, or, better yet, spread them out over a light table and inspect them with a lupe.

The first thing you should be looking for is how good the slides look overall. If your exposures are consistently good, if the focus is clear and the color is coming out well, you know that the way you're shooting your photos is working, and you can go on to look for the finer qualities in your slides. If you aren't getting consistently good results, you'll have to find out why.

Common Problems — If your slides are consistently too dark, you're underexposing them. If they're too light and washed out, you're overexposing them. If the image is blurred, you're jiggling the camera as you press the shutter, or your subject is moving, or your shutter speed is too slow. If you can't figure out what the problem is, it's a good idea to buy a roll or two of film and experiment with exposures, shutter speeds, and lighting conditions, carefully recording how you shot each slide. Check the results against your notes and you should have a good idea of what is happening to your photos.

If you find yourself generally frustrated with the results of your photos, find a beginning photography book and go through it carefully, checking your knowledge of photography against the book; it's good practice for any photographer. There are many excellent, simple, and easy to understand photography books available in camera and book stores and libraries. Textbooks used in basic photo classes in college can be especially helpful to the amateur. (See bibliography.)

But if most of your slides are coming out satisfactorily, then you can direct your attention to the more subtle details of your slides.

Criteria for Editing — First, if you are editing a roll of slides on a light table with a lupe, throw away the obviously unuseable ones—the dark, blurry or washed-out ones. Also discard the ones that have tilted images. Check closely to see that all of your subject is on the slide, that you didn't cut it off at the top, bottom, or sides. Make sure the subject fits comfortably into the frame and isn't overwhelmed by too much space around it, by too many background details, or by a distracting film box or camera strap that was inadvertently left in the frame when you shot the picture.

After you've thrown away the unuseable slides, inspect those you have left. If you've taken more than one slide of each subject, or if you have bracketed your exposures, select the one that seems the very best—the clearest, sharpest, and truest in color. Put it in a stack of your best shots, and put your second choice into a separate pile. Retain the best slide of each piece for your files and use the duplicate or second shots to enter shows, to send to colleges, or to give to artist or design registry files.

If you know at the time you're taking the pictures that you're going to need several slides of the same piece, take the extra shots then rather than later duplicating the number you need from one good original. There are two reasons for doing it this way: you get better quality and it costs less.

Marking Slides — After you have sorted your slides and separated them into groups, mark each slide with the important information about the piece and write or stamp your name on the back of the mount. This will improve the chances for the slide to be returned to you if you send it to a photo lab, a friend, or a competition.

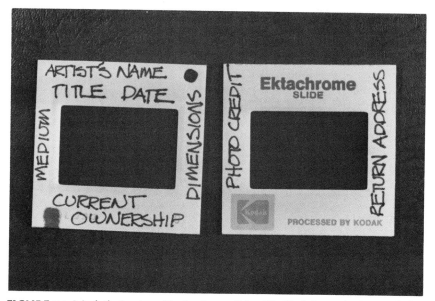

FIGURE 74. *Mark the fronts and backs of your slides. The black dot on the front of the left slide shows the proper way to view the image when it's in the upper right-hand corner. The mark at the opposite corner shows when correctly placed in a carousel tray.*

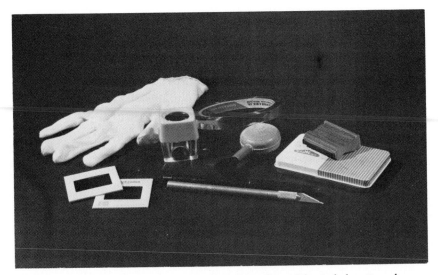

FIGURE 75. *Tools for marking, masking, and handling slides include cotton gloves, a magnifying lupe, metallic mylar tape, a dust brush, an X-acto knife, and a rubber stamp and ink pad. The photographer's name is on the rubber stamp.*

Slide Files

Each slide file system has advantages, and it's a simple matter to decide which method will best suit your purposes.

Carousel or projector box storage is great for teachers or lecturers who show the same slides in the same order every time. You keep one set of slides for each lecture that you give regularly. As long as you don't have to look for a single slide, this is a great system. But, it's not a workable system if you have to pull hundreds of slide slots looking for a single image.

Boxing slides in plastic or metal file boxes is equally as inconvenient a method, unless you're just storing the slides for long periods of time. When packing slides in boxes for long-term storage, slip a packet of silicone crystals into the box to absorb any moisture that could damage the film emulsions.

Keeping slides in the same box that the lab sent them back in, coding the box, and then identifying the subject matter on the outside of the box is a workable system for some people. Since you can only fit thirty-six slides into a film box, you never have more than that many to look through when you're searching for a single slide you know is in a particular box.

Notebook/Slide Page Format — If you have a lot of slides that you want to be able to go through quickly, a notebook/slide page format is about the most convenient file system you can use.

FIGURE 76. Carousel trays will hold 80 or 140 slides. This method of storage is best used by teachers or lecturers who need to keep the slides in a specific order to follow their lecture notes. Artists or designers who have to look for single images, though, should use another filing method.

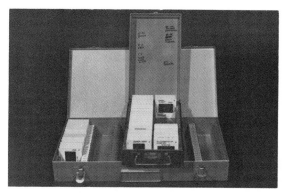

FIGURE 77. Slide storage boxes are good for long term storage, but difficult to use if you need to find a single image quickly.

FIGURE 78. A landscape architect uses this simple boxed storage system for his slides. Each category of slides has a separate box which can hold up to 36 slides.

After editing each roll of slides, you store the ones you want to keep in these vinyl slide pages, organized according to subject matter, the date they were shot, their use, or whichever organizational method you can use.

Each page holds twenty slides that can be scanned quickly over a light table, or up to a lamp or sunny window. Since it takes the eye only a few seconds to scan twenty images, it's possible for an artist or designer to go through an entire slide collection in a few minutes, whereas it would take hours to do the same using other file systems. Another distinct advantage of this method is that the slides are better protected in the vinyl sheets than they are when left exposed in boxes.

Proof Sheets — Proof sheets can be filed in a similar way. Each proof sheet is three-hole punched and numbered sequentially (or in code) on the back and inserted into a three-ring binder. Put the negatives in a separate box, envelope, or folder, and mark each set to correspond with the appropriate proof sheet.

To find a particular image, you leaf through the binder of proof sheets, find the number of the proof sheet you need, and look up the

FIGURE 79. *Contact proofsheets are made from black-and-white negatives. From them, you can select the best few images from the roll; and from the original negatives, high quality enlargements can be made. Cropping instructions should be marked on the images on the proofsheet. Special instructions like print size and paper surface should be clearly written on the back of the proofsheet.*

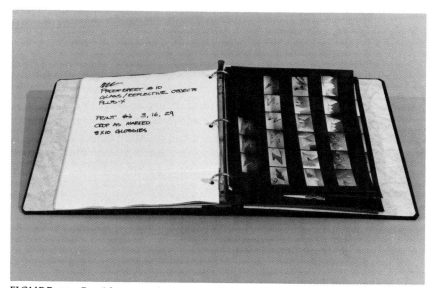

FIGURE 80. *Proofsheets can be conveniently stored in three-ring binders. Each set of negatives is coded to correspond with each proofsheet and stored in a box of negatives. This file system helps you locate the image you're looking for without having to search through all your negatives. Enlarging information or instructions to the photolab can be written on the back of the proofsheet for permanent reference.*

corresponding set of negatives to locate the exact negative you want.

If you carefully replace negatives and slides back in their proper spaces, you should find this file system entirely workable.

Viewing Slides

The 35mm slide image is a bit small for comfortable unaided viewing; it needs to be projected or enlarged in some other way. The many methods of slide enlargement all have their disadvantages—especially in an interview situation. All an artist or designer can do is choose the least awkward of the methods and design his portfolio presentation around it.

Slide Projectors — Although the projected slide probably looks the best of all the methods, the hassle and gymnastics involved in creating an effective slide presentation in someone else's office usually precludes this method of showing your work.

Although conceivably successful in a situation when the artist or designer has plenty of set-up time, space, and a handy projection screen, or when the interviewer comes to the artist's studio and the equipment can be set up in advance, the fact remains that interview situations are rarely so convenient. Add to this the usual nervousness of a typical interviewee, and you can see how easy it would be to make a real fool of yourself if things didn't go like clockwork. Projectors are best left to less-pressured presentations.

Slide Viewers — Another method of showing your slides is to provide a hand-held or desktop viewer that enlarges one hand-inserted slide at a time. The disadvantages of this system are that the slides have to be arranged individually and stacked right-side up, facing the proper direction. A lot of fumbling is usually involved. It's also awkward to operate the viewer, explain the slide, and prepare for the next one simultaneously.

There are more expensive viewers that will accept stacks of slides, which is somewhat more convenient. But there are still problems with these viewers: the interviewer has to be shown how to use the thing, and if a slide in the stack is upside down, there's the hassle of trying to flip it. Again, more fumbling.

Also, since the slides are out of their boxes or page protectors, they're difficult to protect from the viewer's carelessness, and yelling at a potential employer or client for damaging your slides is not going to help you get your job.

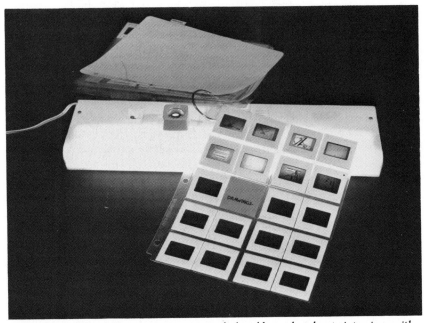

FIGURE 81. *This small and very inexpensive light table can be taken to interviews with a lupe to show slides. Most lupes are available with 8x magnification, which will show about as much detail as an 8 x 10" enlargement of the same slide.*

Slide Pages — In many ways the best solution is to carry your slides in the slide pages discussed previously. With them, carry a lupe and a small, narrow flourescent light box. Sold in hardware stores as an undershelf lighting fixture, this lightweight and surprisingly inexpensive light box will allow you to show as many slides as you want.

You plug the box into a wall socket (make sure the cord is long enough to reach a reasonable distance to an outlet), and give the interviewer your lupe. With a sheet of slides and the light box, he will be able to quickly scan up to twenty images very quickly and then, with the lupe, inspect the slides of interest with more attention. This way you get to show the sharp detail and color of your slides while, at the same time, the interviewer is able to read your markings on each slide, making it simple for him to check size and material information as he sees the image. And you will be using very little of his desktop space.

Though some interviewers may not be used to looking through a lupe, it's not a difficult device to adjust to; a few simple words of instruction from you should do it. For most interview situations, this method is probably the most practical.

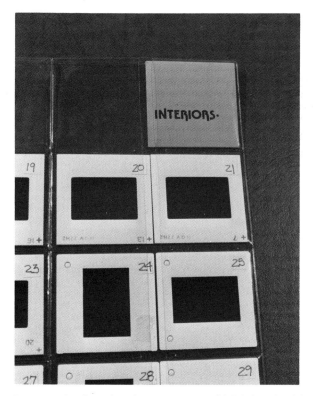

FIGURE 82. *Pieces of colored mat board cut to 2 x 2" and labeled with rubdown lettering make attractive markers for sets of slides.*

Achieving Accuracy with Slides

35mm slides have become a vital part of art, design, and education. They're a versatile, reasonably inexpensive, and perfectly acceptable means of communication in the visual professions. But they're not perfect. The artist and designer who must rely on them to convey information or to document processes must be aware of the problems that slides pose.

First, anything that is large will lose some detail when it's reduced to a 35mm size. Very detailed, elaborate, or delicate artwork, is bound to lose much more than work that's bright, bold, and simple. On pieces where texture is important, it's difficult to accurately capture the tactile qualities that are readily apparent in the original. Very gentle changes in color or value are often lost in slides, as are delicate nuances in line and shading.

It would be foolish to alter your original work just to make more appealing slides, so all an artist or designer can do is to live with the problem and learn to take slides that are of highest possible quality and that capture as much of the subtlety of their work as possible.

Handling Slides Properly

Even if you take very good care of your slides, someone else who looks at them may not. There are, however, a few methods you can use to help protect slides against the gross negligence of others.

Slides and negatives are nothing more than chemical coatings of various colors and thicknesses on strips of acetate. These coatings are very delicate and easily damaged.

Fingerprints on film are permanent; the oil from fingers etches the emulsion of the film and permanently alters the image. A film cleaner may be able to remove the oil residue from a fingerprint, but it can never undo the etching process. Never touch a slide or negative with your bare hands. If you must handle the film, use cotton gloves, which are sold in photo stores for this purpose.

Dust and dirt can accumulate on slides and reduce their quality. Most dirt and dust can be removed with film cleaner and the proper tissue, or by blasting the film with spray from an aerosal can of compressed air. Both of these supplies are carried by photo stores.

Light and heat have more permanent effects on the colors on slides. All slides fade and change with age, but exposing them to strong light or heat accelerates this aging process and drastically reduces the life of the slide. Never leave a slide in a projector longer than necessary. Consider, too, that if any of your slides are ever included in a continuous slide presentation—either in a museum, display, or gallery exhibit that might run continuously for several hours a day— you would be wise to use duplicate slides and to keep the originals stored or filed safely. The constant light and heat of a programmed slide projector can quickly reduce the quality of your slides.

Color Prints

Having color prints made can be frustrating because there are several ways to order them, each of which has its own set of advantages and disadvantages, and none of which gives consistently satisfactory results. Still, color prints are necessary for most portfolios. You'll be able to select the best process for your requirements by knowing more about what's available.

Negative-To-Print — The typical way to have color prints made is to shoot with a color print film. Kodacolor and Vericolor are good standards. From these negatives you can have enlarged color prints made and expect pretty good color representation. The disadvantage of this method is that you need to have small prints made from the negatives first before you can tell which ones you want blown up to portfolio size. Your procedure should go something like black and white film processing:

Shoot the film and send it to a photo lab for processing. Ask for a contact sheet from the negatives. Go over the proof sheet carefully and select those images of which you want large prints, and return the negatives to the lab with the contact sheet and instructions. This is the method commercial photographers use.

Slide-To-Print — With improved photo technology, two other color print procedures have become popular, especially among artists and designers who need slides and color prints in their professions. They are "R" type and Cibachrome processes. In both, the print is made directly from a slide transparency instead of from a negative. Therefore, the intermediate step of having a snapshot made from each negative is eliminated. Looking at a roll of slides with a projector or viewer (or on a light table), the artist can select the image he wants enlarged without having to match snapshots to negatives; he is working directly with the image he wants so there is little chance of getting the wrong negative enlarged. Using either of these processes, your procedure goes something like this:

Shoot a roll of slide film (Ektachrome is a good standard). Send it in for processing. Inspect each of the slides and select the best for enlarging. Send the slides back with your enlarging instructions. Your enlargements and slides are returned.

The quality loss in the slide-to-print method can be controlled somewhat by choosing one technique over another. "R" type prints usually have less contrast than Cibachrome prints. They pick up midrange values well and have an overall soft look to them. Cibachrome colors tend to be very rich and almost sparkling, given a good original slide. But then too, they can be too contrasty and some detail disappears completely. Cibachrome colors are supposed to be the more permanent of the two.

Another slide-to-print method is the "C" print. This technique involves making a negative from the slide and then making a print from the negative. It's more complicated and expensive than any of the other methods. It's most successful application is when it is used to get a reasonably good quality print from a poor quality slide. Negatives are easier to print from and have more latitude in quality control than slides. If you have a good quality slide, however, this technique isn't usually necessary.

If you can't decide which approach will give you the results you need, do your own experimenting. Take a single piece of artwork, shoot it with both kinds of film, and send the same slides and negatives to several labs with the same instructions. Compare the results and decide which method and which lab works best for you. Keep in mind that each of the processes will work, given the proper handling.

The success of your color prints inevitably comes down to two basic factors: the skill with which you are shooting your pictures, and the care given to your work by the color photo lab. If you stop to take the time to run a few tests on these techniques, and then select the process and lab that gives you good results, you won't feel as though you are getting "taken." You'll usually find that good quality costs more, and you'll discover that it's worth it.

Index

(continued from back cover)

HOW TO DO ARCHITECTURAL INK RENDERING by Dennis McBride. Victorian, Gothic and current architectural styles are rendered with a step-by-step technique that makes this a complete instruction manual on the methods, materials and processes of architectural ink rendering. 28 pp., 28 illus. & line drawings, 8 x 10". $2.50.

The following Arthur Baker books are each 8½ x 11", 122 pages, 61 pp. of illus., $12.50/Cloth; $8.95/Paper.

CALLIGRAPHIC INITIALS displays an extensive and innovate series of freely calligraphed initial letters, stressing good design and combined use with type.

DANCE OF THE PEN transforms the letters of the alphabet into abstract imagery and expands the alphabet's graphic design possibilities. For students and art, design and lettering professionals.

THE SCRIPT ALPHABET contains 61 examples of calligraphic script variations—the largest, most unique collection in existence—for all involved in calligraphy.

THE ROMAN ALPHABET by Arthur Baker. Presents 60 new alphabets ranging from traditional to modern, and making use of soft quill pen, split pen and brush strokes. 128 pp., oversize 9 x 12", 62 pp. of illus., clothbound. $15.00.

DESIGN ELEMENTS, Volumes I and II, by Richard and Mies Hora. These highly contemporary, artistically excellent volumes contain a wide-ranging assembly of variations on the most commonly used visual symbols and geometric forms, superbly designed and rendered for reproduction. The first two volumes of a new Annual that will become the visual professional's most prized and utilized resource of high quality clip art. Volume I: circles, spirals, whirls, spheres, optical designs, solar and moon shapes, triangles, star variations, and much more. Volume II: arrows, hand pointers, bursts and banners, hearts, myriad natural shapes, etc., plus a general section with a large variety of symbols from boomerangs to atomic designs. Each volume: 128 pp., over 1,100 illus., exquisitely printed on 80 lb. dull coated stock, casebound. $19.50 per volume; $37.50 for the set of 2 volumes.

TRADEMARKS/VOLUMES 1 through 7, edited by David E. Carter. The acknowledged annuals of trademark design, this series is the standard reference for trademarks. Each volume shows over 1,100 outstanding examples of American symbols, corporate trademarks and logos. A wonderful source and guide for designers of symbols, creative directors, and corporate executives. Each volume: over 220 pp., 8½ x 9½", leather-like cover, casebound, over 1,100 illus. Vol.'s 1 to 3/$14.50 each; Vol.'s 4 to 7/$16.50 each.

Write for a complete catalog:
ART DIRECTION BOOK COMPANY
10 East 39th Street, New York, N.Y. 10016

MAGAZINES

GRAPHIC ARTS BUYER is for buyers of
advertising materials, services and supplies.
Reports the latest news on paper, typography,
lithography, color separations, negatives, direct
mail, etc. Bi-monthly, $9.00/year; $16.00/2 years.

ADVERTISING TECHNIQUES analyzes current
advertising campaigns from idea to finish with
emphasis on the visual. Reports the choice of art,
photography, design, typography, illustration, etc.
to achieve each campaign's concept. Ten issues
annually. $8.50/year; $15.50/2 years.

ART DIRECTION is the field's news
Reports the best and most innovative work in
current advertising, design, photography,
typography, illustration, etc. Each monthly issue
also contains in-depth reports on key people,
events, upcomers, business activities, book
reviews, agency news, and complete award and
trade show information—with many pages in full
color. $18.00/year; $33.00/2 years.